ADHD Reality & Fiction

ADHD Reality & Fiction

*A comprehensive view of ADHD
diagnostics and treatment*

Dr. Alon Avisar

Table of Contents

Acknowledgments

I would like to express my gratitude to the people who believed in me and in my academic and educational practices. I would also like to express my appreciation to the staffs of Sapir College, where I obtained my Bachelor's degree and Tel Aviv University where I received my Master's and my Ph.D. degrees. In particular, I would like to express sincere gratitude to Prof. Daphne Joel for supervising my master's thesis and Prof. Lilac Shalev for supervising my Ph.D. dissertation. Thanks to my wife Einat who illustrated the cover of the book and to my two lovely daughters, Rona and Galia. Special thanks to my parents Amnon and Shoshana who taught me to believe in myself and to be able to face challenges and to dare to see and to express what I see authentically.

Introduction

I was first exposed to Attention-Deficit-Hyperactivity-Disorder (ADHD) in the 2000s when I was working as an educational psychologist at the Educational Psychological Service. I realized that many children were referred there for psychological evaluation due to difficulties in attention and concentration particularly in the learning domain. Having completed their psychological diagnoses, many of the children were then referred for further neurological or psychiatric evaluation in order to determine whether their difficulties in attention and concentration stemmed from ADHD. At that time educational psychologists were not considered sufficiently qualified to diagnose and classify ADHD.

In my career as an educational psychologist, I saw that ADHD manifests, among other things, as difficulty in paying attention to the material under study, difficulty in completing assignments, and a low frustration threshold —all of which lead to impaired functioning and achievement whose outcome is that children with ADHD do not realize their full potential. Emotionally, this failure causes such frustration that self-confidence and self-image decline along with children's motivation. This state of emotional deterioration produces avoidance of action and becomes the source of behavioral problems. I have learned that ADHD is sometimes accompanied by difficulties in social interaction and may lead to the development of anti-social behavior. For this reason, it is important to identify and treat it as soon as possible.

As an educational psychologist, I also have learned that there are two different subtypes of ADHD: ADHD with hyperactivity and impulsivity and ADHD without hyperactivity and impulsivity, which was previously known as ADD. The first subtype is more characterized by behavioral problems, irritability and social difficulties while the second is more characterized by day-dreaming and internalized difficulties. Children with the "ADD" subtype are usually more adept at social functioning than children with the ADHD hyperactivity subtype.

At that time, a mother of a child with ADHD asked me: "How can it be that my child loves video games and is good at playing them." it was hard for me to give her a good answer. My answer at the time was (according to the myth) that children with ADHD can sometimes actually over-focus. However, I was bothered by this since it didn't make sense to me.

As a professional psychologist many questions came to mind: What are the cognitive and neurological mechanisms causing ADHD? How does drug treatment work? Are the different behavioral symptoms in ADHD and ADD (inattention versus hyperactivity and impulsivity) caused by different mental mechanisms? How does drug treatment affect each of these subtypes? Is drug treatment more effective for attention deficit symptoms than it is for hyperactivity and impulsivity symptoms?

My Ph.D. dissertation was an investigation of possible mental and cognitive differences that cause the two different subtypes of behavioral symptoms (inattention vs. hyperactivity and impulsivity) associated with ADHD. With the dedicated assistance of my mentor, Prof. Lilac Shalev, I designed a variety of cognitive tests to measure various mental functions in children with ADHD (Tsal, Shalev, & Mevorach, 2005). Young adults with ADHD were measured on selective attention, orienting attention, arousal and sustained attention, executive attention and executive functions as response inhibition in order to examine the particular relations among these various mental functions and the different behavioral symptoms of inattention, hyperactivity and impulsivity. The working assumption was that specific behavioral symptoms associated with inattention would correlate more with selective attention, orienting attention and/or sustained attention function deficits as accords with Douglas's theory (Douglas, 1972; see chapter 3). While the specific ADHD symptoms associated with hyperactivity and impulsivity would correlate more with executive attention and response inhibition function deficits which belong to the category of executive functioning as accords with Barkley's Theory (Barkley, 1997; see chapter 3).

At the onset of my research, I realized that the subject of ADHD contained a great deal of complexity. This was apparent from detecting and recruiting people who had been diagnosed with ADHD or with suspected ADHD. They all demonstrated considerable diversity in their symptoms and related co-morbidities, along with inclusive mental and cognitive differences. This complexity is inherent to contradictions in basic theories that remain unresolved to this day.

In addition, I realized that the vast research and the clinical findings regarding ADHD do not always match the knowledge of educators and professionals in the field. And as a result, there are many myths about ADHD with regard to educational approaches, diagnostic processes and the treatment. As part of my professional work, I have promoted knowledge about ADHD among psychologists, educators, parents and others in the educational system.

The aim of this book is to align the knowledge in the field with the research and to disprove prevailing myths about ADHD. The book brings together extensive and important information on the subject of what is ADHD, what are its defining characteristics, what are the accepted valid diagnostic processes, what are the limitations upon the diagnosis and the rejection of an ADHD diagnosis by distinguishing attention and concentration difficulties that are the result of other disorders, what is the etiology of ADHD, what are the presentations of cognitive, mental and brain structures and functions that are assumed to underline ADHD, and what are the treatments and interventions.

This information has been obtained through theories and findings developed from studies in the cognitive and neuropsychological field: studies of brain imaging and brain function, heredity, genetics and the environment. The topic of ADHD treatment includes common drug treatments: the types of medications and their composition, how they work, and their effectiveness in treating ADHD and under what conditions and non-drug treatments which include therapeutic interventions and recommendations as well as the non-medical approach which considers temperament and characteristics of people with ADHD as weaknesses and strengths depending on the type of environment and different situations.

The last chapter presents common myths associated with ADHD in order to better understand the disorder and the ways of treating it. The debate converges on how ADHD has become the most commonly diagnosed drug-treated disorder among children in the Western world. What are the likely causes and factors that have led ADHD to become a social and a cultural phenomenon? This leads to the over arching question of whether the ADHD phenomenon has an educational and emotional cost with respect to the development of children.

Chapter 1

Definition and diagnosis

Attention-Deficit/Hyperactivity Disorder (ADHD) is characterized by persistent patterns of inattention and/or hyperactivity-impulsivity that interfere with functioning or development. According to the Diagnostic and Statistical Manual of Mental Disorders, 5th edition (DSM-V, American Psychiatric Association, 2013) the symptoms appear in childhood and continue into adulthood. The DSM-V states that ADHD is characterized by two distinct subtypes of symptoms: Nine describing inattention and nine describing hyperactivity-impulsivity. For a diagnosis of ADHD in childhood, at list six out of the nine symptoms in either type (inattention or hyperactivity-impulsivity), must be met. With older adolescents (ages 17 and older) and adults, at least five symptoms in either type must be met.

These symptoms must persist for at least six months and to a degree that is inconsistent with the child's developmental level and negatively impact social and academic/occupational activities. It is important to verify that the symptoms are not solely a manifestation of oppositional behavior, defiance, hostility, or failure to understand tasks or instructions.

A list of ADHD symptoms according to the DSM-V:

Inattention	Hyperactivity-impulsivity
a. Often fails to give close attention to details or makes careless mistakes in schoolwork, or at work, or during other activities (e.g., overlooks or misses details, work is inaccurate).	a. Often fidgets with or taps hands or feet or squirms in seat.
b. Often has difficulty sustaining attention in tasks or play activities (e.g., has difficulty remaining focused during lectures, conversations, or lengthy reading).	b. Often leaves seat in situations when remaining seated is expected (e.g., leaves his or her place in the classroom, in the office or another workplace, or in other situations that require remaining in place).
c. Often does not seem to listen when spoken to directly (e.g., mind seems to be focused elsewhere, even in the absence of any obvious distraction).	c. Often runs about or climbs in situations where it is inappropriate. (Note: In adolescents or adults, may be limited to feeling restless.)
d. Often does not follow through on instructions and fails to finish schoolwork, chores, or duties in the workplace (e.g., starts tasks but quickly loses focus and is easily sidetracked).	d. Often unable to play or engage in leisure activities quietly.
e. Often has difficulty organizing tasks and	e. Is often "on the go," acting as if "driven by a motor" (e.g., is

activities (e.g., difficulty managing sequential tasks; difficulty keeping materials and belongings in order; messy, disorganized work; has poor time management; fails to meet deadlines).	unable to be or uncomfortable being still over an extended time, as in restaurants, meetings; may be experienced by others as being restless or difficult to keep up with).
f. Often avoids, dislikes, or is reluctant to engage in tasks that require sustained mental effort (e.g., schoolwork or homework; for older adolescents and adults, preparing reports, completing forms, reviewing lengthy papers).	f. Often talks excessively.
g. Often loses things necessary for tasks or activities (e.g., school materials, pencils, books, tools, wallets, keys, paperwork, eyeglasses, mobile telephones).	g. Often blurts out an answer before a question has been completed (e.g., completes people's sentences; cannot wait for his/her turn in a conversation).
h. Is often easily distracted by extraneous stimuli (for older adolescents and adults, may include unrelated thoughts).	h. Often has difficulty waiting for his/her turn (e.g., while waiting in line).

i. Is often forgetful in daily activities (e.g., doing chores, running errands; for older adolescents and adults, returning calls, paying bills, keeping appointments).	i. Often interrupts or intrudes on others (e.g., butts into conversations, games, or activities; may start using other people's things without asking or receiving permission; for adolescents and adults, may intrude into or take over what others are doing).

According to these symptoms three ADHD presentations are possible:

1. <u>ADHD predominantly inattentive presentation</u>: Characterized by Six or more symptoms of inattention for children, or five or more for older adolescents and adults (age 17 and older). But less than six (or five for adults) symptoms of hyperactivity-impulsivity, in the last six months.
2. <u>ADHD predominantly hyperactive-impulsive presentation</u>: Characterized by Six or more symptoms of hyperactivity-impulsivity for children, or five or more for older adolescents and adults (age 17 and older). But less than six (or five for adults) symptoms of inattention, in the last six months.
3. <u>ADHD Combined presentation</u>: Characterized by both: Six or more symptoms of inattention for children, or five or more for older adolescents and adults (age 17 and older). And six or more (or five for adults) symptoms of hyperactivity-impulsivity, in the last six months.

In addition, the following conditions must be met:
- The presence of several inattentive or hyperactive-impulsive symptoms prior to age twelve

- The presence of several inattentive or hyperactive-impulsive symptoms in two or more settings (e.g., at home, school, or work; with friends or relatives; in other activities)
- Clear evidence that the symptoms interfere with or reduce the quality of social, academic, or occupational functioning
- The symptoms do not exclusively occur during episodes of schizophrenia or any other psychotic disorder and are not better explained by another mental disorder (e.g., mood disorder, anxiety disorder, dissociative disorder, personality disorder, substance intoxication or withdrawal).

If the diagnosis of ADHD is conclusive, there are criteria of severity:

1. Mild: Few, if any, symptoms in excess of those required to make the diagnosis and symptoms result in only minor functional impairment
2. Moderate: Symptoms or functional impairment between "mild" and "severe"
3. Severe: Many symptoms in excess of those required to make the diagnosis, or several symptoms that are particularly severe or the symptoms result in marked impairment in social or occupational functioning.

The expression of ADHD at various stages of development across life

Hyperactive behavior is more pronounced among toddlers, although until age four, due to the different kinds of hyperactive expression and the diversity of personality characteristics at this stage it's hard to make a definitive diagnosis. In any case, by kindergarten, the hyperactivity-impulsivity presentation is more evident.

In elementary school when there is a demand for sustained mental effort, attention difficulties are much more pronounced. At this stage, ADHD inattentive presentations and especially combined presentations are more evident. In adults presentations of inattention, planning difficulties and impulsivity are common. Yet, there is considerable decline in symptoms of hyperactivity. Thus, the ADHD inattentive presentation is more common at this stage.

The combined ADHD presentation is the most common overall. It peaks in elementary school and declines in adulthood. The inattentive presentation is the most common among adults. The hyperactivity-impulsivity presentation is the least common overall and appears mostly at the kindergarten stage.

Some people with ADHD show different presentations across a lifespan. Some diagnosed as ADHD hyperactive-impulsive before elementary school are diagnosed with a combined ADHD presentation during elementary school since symptoms of inattention are evident. As adults they will be diagnosed as ADHD inattentive, since hyperactivity declines (Willcutt et al., 2012).

Gender differences

ADHD is more commonly diagnosed in males as compared to females. Gender ratios vary by country ranging from 3:1 to 1.6:1. The gender ratio in ADHD diagnoses decreases with age, although it is still present in adults aged 19 years and over.

Girls with ADHD may be up to twice as likely as boys to have ADHD inattentive presentations and may suffer more from internalizing symptoms and inattention in contrast to the hyperactive and aggressive symptoms exhibited by boys. The difference in ADHD presentations between boys and girls may explain the lower prevalence of ADHD in females. However, regardless of differences in presentation, there are no differences from a standpoint of gender in the essentials of the disorder and its implications (Goldstein & Gordon, 2003).

Cultural differences

There are significant differences in prevalence of ADHD among countries and cultures. The Western world and particularly the United State has the highest prevalence, ranging between 8-12% of the population While, there are other places in which the prevalence rates are much lower (Biederman & Faraone, 2005).The explanation is probably due to differences in measurement and to subjective attitudes toward behavioral symptoms in different cultures. In addition, differences in attitudes regarding educational perceptions, achievement, medical treatments and views of normality among cultures may also contribute to the different prevalences.

How the diagnosis is performed

The professionals certified in diagnosing ADHD are medical psychiatrists, medical neurologists and medical developmental physicians with proper training in diagnosing ADHD. Certified psychologists with special training in diagnosing ADHD are allowed to diagnose provided they refer cases to a certified physician for further medical treatment.

The diagnostic procedure is performed via a clinical interview in order to determine the presence of symptoms and criteria of ADHD according to the diagnostic manual (DSM-V or the International Classification of Diseases (ICD) which is similar to the DSM. Therefore, either the Diagnostic and Statistical Manual of Mental Disorders (DSM) or the international Classification of Diseases (ICD) are suitable for making a diagnosis. The essential thing in making a correct diagnosis is to verify that the symptoms and the criteria are present according to one of the abovementioned manuals.

Hence, theoretically a certified professional could use only one of these manuals for making an appropriate diagnosis.

However, the diagnostic manual (DSM-V) is used for diagnosing ADHD according to its symptoms and certain criteria, In addition the DSM-V indicates that there are several other disorders (detailed in Chapter 2)in which difficulties in maintaining attention appear and the similarity of symptoms may lead to misdiagnosis. These other disorders can show behavioral expressions similar to ADHD and therefore could be diagnosed by mistake as ADHD. Thus, in relying only on symptoms and criteria inquiries, information regarding a different diagnosis could be missed.

To avoid this, other useful tools which serve (as an aid) in obtaining a correct ADHD diagnosis are employed although they are not mandated.

In general, the standard for diagnosing ADHD (according to the Israeli Ministry of Health, circular no. 40/2010) includes not only the clear presence of symptoms and criteria of ADHD according to the diagnostic manual (DSM-V) [or according to the International Classification of Diseases ICD. but also:

A comprehensive developmental interview, a comprehensive clinical interview which rules out other disorders that may mimic the symptoms, parental and teacher questionnaires and interviews about the presence of symptoms of ADHD and the functioning in different environments. Other utilities such as computerized attention tests, psychological, didactic, neuropsychological tests and tests of learning abilities may also be used. These additional examinations for diagnosing ADHD are imported in order to get a more comprehensive and precise diagnosis as well as to rule out other disorders which may explain the symptoms and, thus, to avoid an incorrect diagnosis. It also enables better understanding of the level of severity and the extent of the disability in functioning.

Other important diagnostic tools are:

- As an initial aid, it is highly recommended to perform a comprehensive psycho-didactic or neuropsychology evaluation which examines cognitive ability, learning ability, learning disorders, emotional states, social state, attention and the relations among these domains. This evaluation allows a complete picture of a child's strengths and difficulties to emerge. It can help determine whether the observed inattention symptoms are due to ADHD or to a different source. If the evaluation indicates the likelihood of ADHD, then a referral to a certified physician who uses the DSM to make a diagnosis must be made.

- A Developmental Interview by a certified professional verifies that the symptoms of the disorder are consistent and were present from an early stage in the individual's life and did not suddenly appear. The interview verifies that the symptoms are present in at least two different environments proving that no environmental cause is the source of the observed symptoms and indicates which factors may, in fact, be the cause of the malfunctioning.

- Questionnaires: another tool for use as an aid for certified professionals are questionnaires. Questionnaires supply valuable information from parents and teachers about a child's behaviors in different environments. For adults it also can be used as a self-report. There are several ADHD questionnaires with different versions depends also on their designation (parents/teachers). For example: Conner questionnaires (Conners, 2008), Achenbach questionnaires (Achenbach & Rescorla, 2001), and Wender Self-reporting questionnaires for adults (WURS; Ward, Wender, & Remherr, 1993). These questionnaires detail symptoms and criteria that are part of the psychiatric Diagnostic Manual (DSM) diagnosis and detail behaviors that are directly or indirectly associated with ADHD. They provide additional information on behavior and functioning from different viewpoints and environments. For example, a parent questionnaire contains items about a child's difficulties in sitting for long periods of time, difficulties in organizing tasks and possessions. Teacher questionnaires contain items about the child's difficulties in waiting his/her turn, excessive talking, and interruptive behavior in class. Itis important to note that these questionnaires examine a wide range of symptoms and behaviors that could indicate other disorders beside ADHD. Thus, their reliability and validity are limited and are not valid tools for diagnosis in and of themselves but only serve as an aid.

- Cognitive and neuropsychological tests measure mental abilities that to some extent are related to ADHD (Seidman, 2006). They provide additional diagnostic tools for measuring the impact of difficulty in functioning. These are:

1. Short-term memory tests consisting of transient auditory information that require concentration to absorb information. A person with inattention finds it difficult to absorb transient information.
2. Fine motor tests that usually focus on copying. The assumption is that someone with difficulty in planning and organizing (part of the symptoms of ADHD according to the DSM) will produce inaccurate and sloppy outcomes. Evidence shows that people with ADHD perform more poorly on fine motor tests as compared to people without ADHD (Pitcher, Piek, & Hay, 2003).

3. Specific attention tests: (paper) tests designed to find and circle a target figure located among distractors as fast and as accurately as possible or tests designed to continue lines according to an ordered ascending digit or letter. The assumption is that difficulty in attention or focusing impair the ability to detect the targets quickly and accurately. It must be noted that there are significant differences among persons with ADHD on these tests. Not everyone with ADHD has difficulty with some or all of these tests (Seidman, 2006).

   As mentioned, not everyone with ADHD experiences difficulty on cognitive tests nor does everyone with ADHD exhibit poor performance on memory, fine motor or attention tests. These tests are not definitive in and of themselves and only serve as tools to strengthen a diagnosis, determine its severity or to dismiss a diagnosis if there is doubt concerning some criteria or arising from marginal symptoms.

4. Computerized tests such as the Test of Variable Attention (TOVA) (Greenberg, 1996), Continuous Performance Tests (CPT) (Hall, Valentine, Groom, Walker, & Sayal, 2016) and CPT-MOXO (Berger & Cassuto, 2014) are also used as an aide in diagnosing ADHD. Although the tests vary in length and type of stimuli used, the basic nature of the tests is to present subjects with a repetitive, boring task over the course of 15–20 minutes and require them to maintain their focus during this time in order to respond to targets or to inhibit a response to foils. Although the tests may use numbers, symbols, or even sounds, the basic task has the same concept. The procedure in these tests is as follows: on the computer screen a sequence of stimuli appears one after the other. The subject is

instructed to respond to the appearance of certain geometric shapes by pressing a responder button and to inhibit clicking when presented with other geometric shapes, for example, to press when the letter "X" appears and not when the letters "A, V, Z, S" appear. The tests vary in stimulus intervals, speed, type of symbols, target/non-target ratio etc. However, the basic nature of these tests remains the same. The recent version of the CPT-MOXO adds visual and auditory background interference into the test in order to measure the influence of background noise on subjects.

In all the different versions of the CPT, the main measure is variability of reaction time or the mean variability of the amount of time between the presentation of the stimulus and the subject's response. If a subject responds to the target one time quickly and another time slowly, it equates to higher variability and poorer performance as compared to responses with consistent speed.

Omission errors indicate the number of times the subject did not respond (click the mouse) when presented with the target. High omission rates indicate that the subject is either not paying attention to stimuli or has a sluggish response.

Commission errors indicate the number of times the subject responded but no target was presented. Fast reaction times and high commission error rate point to impulsivity. Slow reaction times and high commission and omission errors indicate inattention.

It was found that people with ADHD exhibit poorer performance on these computerized attention tests than people without ADHD. Their poorer performance is reflected in all measures on all versions of the test. Since these tests involve low-level cognitive load, they mostly measure the ability to sustain attention or concentration over a long period of time. They are also supposed to measure impulsivity, although there is some controversy over whether they actually do so.

It is important to note that not all people with ADHD exhibit poor performance on these tests. Conversely, people without ADHD as well as people with other disorders exhibit poor performance on these tests. Thus, these tests cannot serve as the main diagnostic tool, but only as an aid. The only valid ADHD diagnosis once again is that done according to the DSM manual by a certified professional. If this professional needs further proof of the presence of the disorder, these tests can help validate or reject the diagnosis.

Another use of these computerized tests is to test the effectiveness of the medication. It has been found that people with ADHD who are on medication exhibit improvement in their performance (Riccio, Waldrop, Reynolds, & Lowe, 2001).

Chapter 2

The distinctions between attention difficulties resulting from ADHD and attention difficulties resulting from other disorders

The first question we should ask is: does anyone who has difficulties with attention and concentration have ADHD? Absolutely not! Difficulties with attention are not exclusive to ADHD. In fact, there are numerous disorders in which attention difficulties appear; not to mention that almost any uncomfortable situation can lead to lack of attention, nervousness or irritability. A headache or lack of sleep can produce concentration problems and irritability. How can anyone be expected to concentrate or learn when their head is throbbing with pain or after a disconcerting incident that that continues to percolate through the mind?

The diagnostic manual (DSM-V), which defines ADHD according to specific symptoms and criteria indicates that there are several other disorders in which attention difficulties appear and their behavioral expressions are so similar to those of ADHD that a mistaken diagnosed of ADHD could be made.

The emotional and psychiatric disorders include depression, anxiety, bipolar (manic depression), emotional regulation, and interpersonal interference. The behavioral disorders are Oppositional Defiant Disorder (ODD) and explosive personality disorders. The developmental disorders consist of learning disorders, autistic spectrum disorder (ASD), and intellectual disabilities. Psychotic conditions, effects of medications, and drug abuse comprise the other disorders (DSM-V, American Psychiatric Association, 2013).

It is important to mention that some of these disorders show comorbidity with ADHD. So, someone could be diagnosed with ADHD and with an additional learning disorder or ODD. However, the endeavor is not to make an incorrect diagnose ADHD due to attention difficulties that are caused by other disorders. Thus, it is crucial to diagnose ADHD according to all the symptoms and criteria mentioned in the DSM-V and to verify that the symptoms of inattention are not the product of other disorders. In other words, the main job of the diagnostician is to verify that the cause of inability to function is due to ADHD and not to some other cause.

Attention and concentration difficulties resulting from emotional and psychiatric disorders

Depression

One of the major symptoms of depression is difficulty to concentrate. Unlike adults, depression in children is characterized more by restlessness, nervousness, difficulty in maintaining attention, reduction in functioning and behavioral problems. Children's periods of depression and their transformation are less consistent than in adults. Thus, differentiation between depression and ADHD is difficult is difficult to discern in children and this can easily lead to an incorrect diagnosis of ADHD (Brunsvold, Oepen, Federman, & Akins, 2008). Thus, it is very important to rule out the impact of depression in reduced functioning when validating an ADHD diagnosis.

Anxiety

Anxiety is characterized by excessive thought and worry. It is generally accompanied by restlessness, problems in concentration, irritability and sleep disturbance. On the physiology level, high levels of arousal and fast heart rates are common.

In children, anxiety appears as inattention, hyperactivity and impulsivity, symptoms similar to ADHD (Jarrett, & Ollendick, 2008; Tannock, 2000). Moreover, as in ADHD, children with anxiety show poor performance on attention tests. They are easily distracted by irrelevant stimuli and have difficulty focusing (Reinholdt-Dunne, Mogg, Vangkilde, Bradley, & Esbjørn, 2015). There is a positive correlation between intrusive thoughts and poor performance on selective attention tests (Avisar, 2011).

Since children with anxiety exhibit symptoms of inattention and hyperactivity along with poor performance on attention tests, it is hard to distinguish between anxiety and ADHD. This could easily lead to an incorrect diagnosis of ADHD. According to the psychiatric manual (DSM), in order to avoid an incorrect diagnosis, it is important to reveal the causes of the symptoms. In anxiety symptoms of inattention and hyperactivity are generated from restlessness and worry whereas, in ADHD, the symptoms are the result of impatience, the reluctance to do tasks that require sustained mental effort and the drive to look for or engage in more exciting activities.

Other emotional and psychiatric disorders

According to the psychiatric manual (DSM), another disorder that demonstrates inattention, hyperactivity and impulsivity is bipolar disorder (manic-depression).In bipolar disorder the cause of the symptoms is emotional. Therefore, the intensity and duration of symptoms vary according to shifting emotional states. This contrasts with the symptoms of ADHD which are more consistent stable. Likewise, Sensory Modulation Disorder also manifests as inattention, nervousness and hyper-activity. However, unlike ADHD the cause of the symptoms is a sensation in the nervous system.

Problems in inter-relationships in children can lead to major distress and as a consequence nervousness and restlessness. Since, ADHD is sometimes accompanied by problems in inter-relationships, a certified professional must determine if the problems in inter-relationships are primary or secondary in order to avoid an incorrect diagnosis of ADHD.

Symptoms of inattention resulting from behavioral difficulties

Although ADHD is often characterized by behavioral difficulties, it often has co-morbidity with Oppositional Defiant Disorder (ODD),the psychiatric Diagnostic and Statistical Manual (DSM-V) emphasizes that behavioral problems characterized by a negative, defiant attitude toward authority and hostile behavior may present with inattention and impulsive symptoms similar to those of ADHD. It was also found that children with ODD and without the co-morbidity of ADHD show poor performance on the computerized Continuous Performance Test (CPT) for assessing attention and impulsive behavior. It was found that these children with ODD and without ADHD exhibit lower brain activity in areas related to executive attention and target identification (Baving, Rellum, Laucht, & Schmidt, 2016). Since, ODD without a co-morbidity of ADHD can manifest inattention and impulsivity and also yield poor performance on computerized attention tests, the DSM-V emphasizes that a diagnosis of ADHD must also verify that these symptoms do not result from the lack of cooperation which characterizes ODD.

Another disorder which shows symptoms similar to ADHD is Intermittent Explosive Disorder. This disorder is characterized by explosive outbursts of anger and violence. However, according to the DSM-V the difference between Intermittent Explosive Disorder and ADHD is that in the former anger is directed at others while in ADHD it is not.

Symptoms of inattention resulting from learning disorders

The psychiatric Diagnostic and Statistical Manual (DSM-V) defines learning disorders as significant learning difficulties and academic skills that are substantially below that expected for the child's age. It refers to ongoing problems in reading, writing and math that are foundational to the ability to learn despite interventions targeting those difficulties. A diagnosis of learning disorder can only obtain if it is not due to other conditions, such as intellectual disability, vision or hearing problems, a neurological condition (e.g., pediatric stroke), adverse conditions such as economic or environmental disadvantage, lack of instruction, or difficulties speaking/understanding the language.

In addition to the substantial learning difficulties, learning disorders cause great distress, emotional difficulty, and a desire to leave the classroom and not engage in learning. As a result, they can lead to inattention and lack of concentration, restlessness and behavioral problems (Bender & Smith, 1990). And it can also lead to social difficulties (Kavale & Forness, 1996).

Accordingly, the psychiatric Diagnostic and Statistical Manual (DSM-V) emphasizes that children with learning disorders and without ADHD can appear inattentive and restlessness. Due to frustration resulting from difficulties in learning, their symptoms only appear in educational environments in contrast to ADHD where inattention appears in at least two different settings. Hence, children with learning disorders can be misdiagnosed with ADHD if the reason for the inattention is not fully analyzed.

Symptoms of inattention resulting from Autism Spectrum Disorder

Autism Spectrum Disorder (ASD) is characterized by difficulty in social communication, social interaction, self-management, regulation of emotions and behavior and inattention. Children with ASD can show some symptoms that mimic those of ADHD.

The DSM-V indicates that the difference between ASD and ADHD is in the origin of the symptoms. In children with ASD, behavioral difficulties, frustration and outbursts of rage appear due to difficulties in making changes and transitions and to difficulties in understanding social situations. By contrast, behavioral problems originating in ADHD are due to impulsivity. ADHD and ASD have specific attention/executive function profiles which refute the idea of a continuum of ADHD-Inattentive, ADHD-Hyperactivity and ASD with increasing cognitive impairment (Boxhoorn et al., 2018).

It should be note that the previous Diagnostic and Statistical Manual (DSM-IV) precluded a simultaneous diagnosis of ASD and ADHD, however, the DSM-V allows ASD and ADHD to be diagnosed together provided that apart from the ASD diagnosis, all criteria and symptoms of ADHD are met.

Symptoms of inattention resulting from other disorders

The DSM-V mentions other disorders like intellectual and developmental disability whose symptoms include inattention and lack of concentration. Accordingly, inattention symptoms are prevalent among children with Intellectual and developmental disability. The symptoms appear in educational frameworks that are above the child's intellectual capacity and less in non-educational environments. If children with intellectual disability are diagnosed with ADHD, their symptoms of inattention, hyperactivity and impulsivity should be highly deviant and exceed their expected mental age.

Other neurodevelopment disorders characterized by repetitive motor behavior can show symptoms of hyperactivity characterized by specific patterns. In ADHD, hyperactivity is more generalized and not characterized by repetition.

In addition, side-effects of drugs or drug abuse can generate difficulties in concentration, restlessness and impulsivity. Psychotic conditions can also generate difficulties in focusing, hyperactivity and impulsivity. Thus, it is important to rule out these conditions before giving an ADHD diagnosis.

Symptoms of inattention resulting from personality disorders

Personality disorders are defined as sustained patterns of internal experiences and inflexible behaviors which appear in many different situations. This pattern of experience which is prone to inflexible interpretation, results in behaviors that deviate from the behavioral norm expected in personal and social situations and significantly impairs functioning in various situations. For example, in borderline personality disorders, the internal experience of idealization, devaluation and inseparability in relationships allows social criticism to cause internal experiences of rejection or self-devaluation. This in turn produces frustration, anger, emotional and behavioral difficulties.

In adolescents and adults it is difficult to distinguishing between personality disorder and ADHD since personality disorder is characterized by disorganization, difficulty in emotional regulation, social and behavioral difficulty and impulsivity. However, in contrast to personality disorder,

ADHD is not characterized by separation anxiety, self-harm and exaggerated ambivalence. In order to distinguish between the two disorders, an emotional analysis that includes a careful interview, observations and a history must reveal the emotional processes underlying the symptoms.

ADHD and co-morbidities

As mentioned, inattention symptoms, hyperactivity and impulsivity can be an outcome of other disorders. Thus, these symptoms are not exclusive to ADHD. However, ADHD can be accompanied by other disorders (co-morbidities of ADHD). Hence, a person with ADHD can diagnosed with additional disorders as well. In order to determine that more than one disorder exists, the full criteria and symptoms of both disorders must appear.

Co-morbidity of ADHD and learning disorders
One of the most prevalent co-morbidities with ADHD is learning disorders. It is estimated that 16-48% of the children with ADHD also have learning disorders (Wei, Yu& Shaver, 2014). Some studies have found that up to 70% of children with ADHD have a learning disorder. The most common learning disorder in ADHD is Written Expression disorder (65%) and its prevalence is double that of reading or arithmetic disorders (previously known as dyslexia and dyscalculia) (Mayes, Calhoun& Crowell, 2000).

However, ADHD is not a learning disorder in and of itself and the underlying mechanisms of ADHD and learning disorders are different, the question remains why the high percent of overlap. Since both ADHD and learning disorders can be inherited. One assumption was that the correspondence (of marriage) between people with ADHD and people with learning disorders is significantly higher than common probability would indicate. Children of parents with these combined disorders will have higher probability of having both ADHD and learning disorders as compared to children whose parents do not have these overlapping disorders. However, some studies refute this assumption and conclude that ADHD and arithmetic disorder are independent of each other and are inherited separately (Monuteaux, Faraone, Herzig, Navsaria, & Biederman, 2005). Moreover, although evidence shows that ADHD and reading disorder can sometimes be transmitted by both parents, reading disorder is also inherited separately and independently from ADHD (O'Neill & Douglas, 1991). Moreover, the significant impairment in language mechanisms (coding, phonological awareness, etc.) found in people with dyslexia are not the main characteristics of ADHD (Roese, Hynd, Knight, Hiemenz, & Hall, 2000).

Although the reason why many children with learning disorders also have ADHD is still unknown, one explanation may be technical: the definition of learning disorder is wide and varies among different studies. Different studies include different variables and different specific learning disorders such as reading, writing, reading comprehension, written expression, arithmetic, educational and functional disparity, etc. Hence, all together these disabilities receive higher percentages of learning disorders in ADHD. A second reason may relate to the levels of severity of ADHD and learning disorders. As levels of severity of both disorders vary among children, the higher percentages of co-morbidities may reflect higher variability among the severities of each disorder, for example, severe ADHD with mild learning disorder and severe learning disorder with mild ADHD, etc. Another reason may be that, although ADHD is not defined as a learning disorder, it often causes learning difficulty and learning malfunction due to concentration difficulties, disorganization, and avoidance of tasks that require continuous mental effort. This may lead to educational gaps and low achievement. People with ADHD can easily be misdiagnosed with learning disorder due to malfunctions in learning. On the other hand, the frustrations of people with learning disorders can cause low levels of motivation, a desire to avoid learning, restlessness and difficulties in concentration which can lead to an incorrect diagnosis of ADHD.

Co-morbidity of ADHD and behavioral disorders

Another common co-morbidity of ADHD is Oppositional Defiant Disorder (ODD). ODD is characterized by a negative attitude and hostile behavior toward authority figures. It is estimated that 40-60% of children with ADHD have ODD. Some of these children show antisocial behavior or are at risk to develop such behavior (Biederman, Newcorn, & Sprich, 1991; Biederman et al., 2000). Research examining the relation between ADHD and ODD finds that symptoms of emotional impulsivity such as outbursts of anger can be present in ADHD but are not integral to it (Factor, Reyes & Rosen, 2014). It has been found that the source of behavioral problems in ODD is early development of negative emotions and anger, not ADHD (Smith, Lee, Martel, & Axelrad, 2017). When comparing presentations of subtypes of ADHD, it has been found that people with ADHD and inattention but without hyperactivity have fewer behavioral problems than people with ADHD and hyperactivity (Gaub & Carlson, 1997; Lahey & Carlson, 1992).

Although ADHD is sometimes perceived as a behavioral disorder, it is not defined as such and behavioral problems are not integral to it. In the DSM-V, ADHD appears under the category of neuro-developmental disorders as opposed to the previous manual version (DSM-IV where ADHD appeared under the category of behavioral disorders.

In order to distinguish between behavioral problems resulting from ADHD and those stemming from behavioral disorder, the cause of the behavioral problems must be detected. Behavioral problems resulting from ADHD are characterized by inattentive encounters, interruptions in class, lawbreaking, failure to adhere to authority and sometimes aggressive behavior due to impatience, quick onset of boredom (mainly in low stimuli environments), recklessness and impulsivity. On the other hand, behavioral disorders which are not due to ADHD are characterized by a basic intention to hurt others due to negative emotions and anger.

Co-morbidity of ADHD and Social difficulties

Another co-morbidity of ADHD is interpersonal difficulty, which is characterized by conflict with teachers, parents and friends and can result in social rejection (Barkley, 1997; Nixon, 2001). Yet, unlike children with communication disorder or non-verbal learning disability, children with ADHD have no impairment in understanding non-verbal social and emotional cues. Children with ADHD (without hyperactivity) with inattention presentations show better social and emotional functioning than children with ADHD with hyperactivity presentations (Semrud-Clikeman, Walkowiak, Wilkinson, & Minne, 2010). Thus, it appears that the social difficulties of people with ADHD are related more to impulsivity and to difficulty in regulating emotions than to social understanding.

Co-morbidity of ADHD and emotional difficulties

Emotional difficulties also have co-morbidity with ADHD. It is estimated that 25-56% of the people with ADHD have emotional difficulties (Wei et al., 2014). With regard to ADHD and depression, it has been reported that 13-27% of the people with ADHD have depression and up to 60% in clinical populations (Regularly treated in therapeutic settings). It was also reported that 5-50% of children with depression also have ADHD. The explanation for the high percentages of comorbidity may be that children with depression show less sadness and more restlessness and lack of concentration, they are sometimes misdiagnosed with ADHD.

Given all the above, the question arises about the complexity of ADHD as a separate diagnosis. This puts into focus the risk of an incorrect diagnosis (Brunsvold et al., 2008). Avisar and Shalev (2009) found that emotional difficulties relate more to behavioral inattention and symptoms of impulsivity as measured by a questionnaire than poor performance on the cognitive computerized attention test (CPT). This proven direct relationship between emotional difficulties and inattention and impulsivity is probably not the result of ADHD.

Summary

As people with ADHD have many co-morbidities, it is of great importance to negate the presence of other disorders in order to obtain a comprehensive assessment of ADHD as the main source of the malfunction. That's because other disorders which directly relate to the malfunctions shows behavioral symptoms similar to ADHD and may be incorrectly diagnosed as a secondary co-morbidities of ADHD. For example, Kube, Petersen, and Palmer (2002) state that young children with learning disorders, emotional and behavioral difficulties, developmental and language delay, communication disorder, Autistic Spectrum Disorder (ASD) and intellectual and developmental disability can be diagnosed incorrectly with ADHD since lack of concentration, inattention and restlessness are common to all these disorders. They further state that evaluations of ADHD are neither comprehensive nor sufficient due to economic considerations, difficulty diagnosing learning disorders at an early age and brief evaluations due to overload and long queues.

Accordingly, adolescents diagnosed with ADHD stated during their interviews that they did not remember much from the evaluation process (also adolescents said that the evaluation process took place in close proximity to their interview). They also stated that they were not told much beyond that they would have to take medicine to help them overcome their difficulties in concentrating. Furthermore, some adolescents asserted that their learning difficulties persisted despite their medication. They required further evaluation for learning disorders and eventually they were identified with learning disorders (Avisar & Lavie, 2014). The adolescent interviews leave the impression that some of the ADHD diagnoses were neither comprehensive nor accurate. Accordingly, it seems that their Learning disorders were not examined as a possible factor in their difficulties. They were misdiagnosed with ADHD although their difficulties in concentration were probably due to frustration in learning.

In reality, because of economical and time constraints questionnaires for detecting ADHD are often use as the only additional aid. Because these questionnaires are not sensitive enough to detect ADHD accurately, they are not reliable (Posserud et al., 2014). The behavioral symptoms that they investigate relate to ADHD but are not exclusive to ADHD and can be found in other disorders. Thus, if other disorders which have similar symptoms as ADHD exist, the possibility exists that these questionnaires produce "false positives" for ADHD. For example, the popular Conners Questionnaire (2008) for the evaluation of ADHD contains items relating to emotional, social difficulties, behavioral and learning difficulties. Thus, although these difficulties are related to ADHD, they are not exclusive to ADHD and appear in many other disorders, so there is a chance for an incorrect diagnosis of ADHD.

The notion that behavioral symptoms of inattention, lack of concentration, impulsivity and motor restlessness are not only not exclusive to ADHD, but are common to other disorders. And the fact that ADHD has many co-morbidities with variable incidences between studies has lead Furman (2005) to doubt the accuracy and consistency of ADHD diagnoses. Furman (2005) further questions whether ADHD exists as a specific disorder or is an assortment of behavioral symptoms stemming from emotional and behavioral difficulties, learning and other disorders and difficulties. The finding that 60% of children diagnosed with ADHD have at least one other disorder such as behavioral problems, anxiety, depression, or ASD (Danielson et al, 2018) strengthens Furman's (2005) assumption that at least in some cases ADHD-like symptoms derive from other disorders.

According to world wide data, ADHD is one of the most common disorders among children even though the diagnostic and statistical psychiatric manual (DSM-V; American Psychiatric Association, 2013) estimates a prevalence of only 5%. Other estimates of prevalence range from 8-12% with high variability among regions, countries and cultures (Biederman & Faraone, 2005). The estimated number of children diagnosed with ADHD in the US according to a 2016 parent survey is 6.1 million (9.4%) (Danielson et al, 2018). In Israel, the prevalence was found to be 9.5% in the Jewish sector (almost 1 to 10 similar to US and other Western countries) and 7.5% in the Arab sector (Ornoy, Ovadia, Rivkin, Milshtein, & Barlev, 2016). The high variability in the world wide data strengthen the assumption of over-diagnosis probably derived from evaluations that are not comprehensive enough. Most likely other disorders were misdiagnosed as ADHD.

Chapter 3

Etiology of ADHD

According to the current Diagnostic and Statistical Manual (DSM-V), ADHD is categorized as a neuro-developmental disorder which affects cognitive ability and produces behavioral symptoms of inattention, hyperactivity and impulsivity (American Psychiatric Association, 2013). This is opposed to the previous manual (DSM-IV), in which ADHD was categorized as a behavioral disorder.

In exploring the causes for the neurological and cognitive impairment produced by ADHD, research has focused on three domains:

- *The neuropsychology domain:* Research has focused on impaired cognitive and mental processes by comparing people with ADHD and people without ADHD on cognitive tests (both computerized attention tests and neuro-psychological tests) that examine neuropsychological processes.
- *The brain imaging domain:* Research has focus on finding deficits in brain structures and in activities

indicating brain malfunction in people with ADHD as compared to people without ADHD.

- *The genetics and heredity domain:* Research has focused on the influence of genetics, heredity and the environment on ADHD.

Neuropsychological dysfunction in ADHD

Major studies tried to determine the source deficits underlying behavioral symptoms of ADHD via neuropsychological tests that measure cognitive ability and functioning (intelligence, verbal ability visual processing, memory, attention, executive function, etc.). Both paper and pencil and computerized tests (e.g., TOVA and CPT for attention) were used. Performance on these tests is usually measured in terms of speed and accuracy. The assumption is that slowness or inaccuracy indicate poor cognitive ability.

The question is: what is the basic neuropsychological deficit in ADHD and are the deficits that underly the inattention symptoms distinctly different from deficits that underly the hyperactivity and impulsivity symptoms. It had been assumed that inattention is due to deficits in selective attention-the ability to focus on some target while ignoring distractors – while the symptoms of hyperactivity and impulsivity are due to deficits in inhibition and regulation of behavior which belong to the realm of executive functioning. However, these assumptions were found to be incorrect.

Is a deficit in selective mental attention the main reason for inattention in ADHD?

Since the disorder is characterized by distractibility and difficulty in maintaining attention over long periods of time, the primary explanation for ADHD is that a deficit in cognitive selective attention is responsible for the distractibility and inattention behavioral symptoms.

It is important to clear up the confusion between distractibility in reality (e, g. a person who declares that he/she is distracted or appears to be distracted by the noise or the light in the environment) and the actual cognitive ability to select and focus attention. In other words, not everyone who declares that there is a distraction or appears to be distracted by an environment stimulus has an impairment in the brain's cognitive ability to select and focus attention.

Capability for selective cognitive attention (selectivity, focus, direction) is measured by tests in which the subject is asked to identify a target figure among stimuli that distract attention. While there are many kinds of selective cognition tests, most are visual with the difference among them being the salience of the target figure, the number of distractors, their positioning and compatibility. Speed and accuracy in identification of a target without distractors is compared to speed and accuracy in identifying the same target with distractors. These determine cognitive ability for selective attention.

The basic assumption is that symptoms of inattention in ADHD are due to a deficit in cognitive selectivity. Many studies examining performance on selective cognitive attention tests have found that children with ADHD show lower achievement on these tests than children without ADHD (Brodeur & Pond, 2001; Hazell et al., 1999). However, the findings are not definitive since other studies that employ the same tests did not find significant differences in selective cognitive attention between children and adults with ADHD and children and adults without ADHD (Avisar, 2011; Van der Meere & Sergeant, 1988). Moreover, no significant differences in selective cognitive attention between children with ADHD presentations characterized by inattentive behavior (but without hyperactivity) and children with ADHD presentations characterized by hyperactive presentations (Pritchard, Neumann, & Rucklidge, 2008) were found using these tests. Specifically, symptoms of inattentive behavior in people with ADHD were not found to correlate to selective attention (Avisar, 2011).

Based on these results and others regarding the inconclusive relation between selective attention and ADHD, researchers have emphasized that despite the notion that ADHD is accompanied by behavioral symptoms of inattention, there is insufficient evidence to prove that a deficit in selective attention is the cause of these symptoms (Huang-Pollock, Nigg, & Carr, 2005). Surprisingly, it was found that difficulty in selective mental attention did correlate with anxiety (Reinholdt-Dunne, Mogg, Vangkilde, Bradley, & Esbjørn, 2015), obsessive compulsive disorder (Cohen, Lachenmeyer, & Springer, 2003) and personality traits associated with introversion and neuroticism (Avisar, 2011).

While it may seem contra-intuitive that deficits in selective mental attention are not primary in ADHD and that these deficits do not elicit symptoms of inattention in people with ADHD, theories that once explained deficiencies in selective mental attention as the basis for the behavioral symptoms of ADHD are no longer the center of research in ADHD.

The best simple example of why cognitive selective attention is not the main deficit in ADHD is video games. Years ago, a mother of a child with ADHD asked me: "How can it be that my child loves video games and is good at playing them." At the time it was hard for me to give her a good answer. My answer at the time was (according to the myth) that children with ADHD can sometimes actually over-focus. However, I was bothered by this since it didn't make sense to me.

A lot of children both those with and without ADHD, love and are good at playing video games. Video games require a lot of control and selective cognitive ability in order to move the control panel (joystick) according to the fast-paced events on the computer screen that are accompanied by lots of stimuli and distractors. The fact that children with ADHD have no problem in doing this demonstrates that selective cognitive attention is not the main deficit in ADHD.

Deficits in sustained attention and arousal and response inhibition

One of the early theories in ADHD research claims that the primary mental and cognitive deficit in ADHD is sustained attention and low arousal (Douglas, 1972). The assumption was that low arousal–similar to fatigue–reduces alertness and impairs ability to maintain attention and concentration. However, since people with ADHD are also characterized by behavioral symptoms of low organization, hyperactivity and impulsivity, one of the more recent theories assumes that a deficit in inhibition of cognitive mental response (which is part of executive functioning) is the primary deficit underlying ADHD (Barkley, 1997).

It is important to note the significant differences that exist between the theory of sustained attention and that of response inhibition. Unlike the cognitive function of sustained attention and arousal, response inhibition is considered to be an executive function. However, since the cognitive functions of sustained attention and response inhibition are usually measured by the same test (the Continuous Performance Test (CPT)–consideration of these two cognitive functions will be done together. In order to clarify the relationship between the test and the two theories explaining ADHD, the CPT and its measures will be analyzed.

In the CPT, different stimuli (for example: a red circle, a blue square, a blue circle, and a red square) are presented in sequence. Each time only one image appears on the screen ensuring that the test does not measure ability in selective attention. One stimulus is defined as the target stimulus. The respondent is instructed to press a key only when that stimulus is detected (for example, a red square) and not to press the key when a non-target stimulus appears (for example: a red circle or a blue square). Different versions of the CPT maintain the same concept although the frequency of the target event and other variable may vary. The test has three main measures: (1) *Variation in response time*: Large variance, obtained if a respondent sometimes responds quickly to the onset of the target and at other times responds slowly is indicative of low functioning, while low variance, obtained if a respondent responds at a consistent speed to all target stimuli is indicative of high functioning. (2) *Omission Errors* – cases where the respondent does not respond to the target stimulus or misses the target is indicative of poor functioning. (3) *Commission Errors* - cases where the respondent responds to non-target stimuli also indicates poor functioning. Theoretically, variation in response time and omission errors measure sustained attention and arousal, while commission errors measure response inhibition.

The literature shows that people with ADHD consistently show poor performance on all three measures, sustained attention measures (Hervey, Epstein & Cury, 2004) as well as response inhibition measures (Epstein et al., 2003; Epstein, Johnson, Varia, & Conners, 2001) as compared to people without ADHD.

Accordingly, poor performance of people with ADHD on the sustained attention measures strengthens the theory that sustained attention deficit underlies ADHD, whereas, poor performance of people with ADHD on the response inhibition measures strengthens the theory claiming that deficits in response inhibition underly ADHD. Deficit in response inhibition also provides a logical explanation for the behavioral symptoms of impulsivity and hyperactivity although not for the symptoms of inattention.

Nevertheless, some questioned arise: Why do people with ADHD show poor performance on all CPT measures? Theoretically, this indicates difficulty in both the arousal and the sustained attention cognitive functions as well as difficulty in response inhibition. Additionally, this questions the validity of the response inhibition theory for people with only the inattentive presentation of ADHD.

It had been assumed that symptoms of inattention relate more to difficulties in sustained attention and arousal, whereas, the symptoms of hyperactivity and impulsivity relate more to difficulties in response inhibition (Avisar & Shalev, 2011). As previously mentioned, studies that examined this assumption found that measures of both sustained attention and response inhibition relate equally to behavioral symptoms of both inattention and hyperactivity-impulsivity. In addition, significant correlation between measures of sustained attention and response inhibition were found. This would indicate possible theoretical relations between these measures (Avisar & Shalev, 2011; Epstein et al., 2003). A study published in one of the most prestigious journals in the field found that children with ADHD who showed deficits in sustained attention and arousal also showed high rates of commission errors (response inhibition). Thus, this study conjectures that commission errors are probably due to deficits in sustained attention and arousal rather than to deficits in response inhibition (Johnson et al., 2007). These findings suggest that the basic assumption that deficit in sustained attention and arousal is related to behavioral symptoms of inattention while impairment in response inhibition is related to behavioral symptoms of impulsivity and hyperactivity is fundamentally incorrect.

Moreover, it was found that poor performance on the CPT which theoretically measures sustained attention and response inhibition is not limited to ADHD. It has been found that children with Opposite Defiant Disorder (ODD) and without ADHD also show poor performance on the CPT (Baving, Rellum, Laucht & Schmidt, 2016). In addition, it was found that as physiological anxiety or high arousal increases, response inhibition improves. This strengthens the arousal theory. However, mental (cognitive) anxiety impairs response inhibition on the CPT (Epstein, Goldberg, Conners, & March, 1997). Thus, it appears that difficulties in sustained attention and response inhibition are not exclusive to ADHD. Moreover, no neuropsychological differences were found in the mental functioning of people with the inattentive presentation of ADHD (without hyperactivity) and people with the hyperactivity and impulsivity presentation of ADHD. As research into the causes of ADHD has produced no definitive answers, research into the basic deficits in ADHD has also focused on other impairments in executive functioning.

Neuropsychological deficits in executive functions in ADHD

Numerous findings in the last two decades show that people with ADHD perform poorly on a variety of tests of executive functions (Yang et al., 2011). Executive functions which includes: the ability to plan, organization, flexibility of thought, focus on goals, working memory, behavioral and emotional regulation, response inhibition and more. These functions are measured using both computerized and pen and paper tests that measure response time and accuracy in the manipulations being tested.

A meta-analysis by a respected researcher in this field (Seidman, L.) has gathered all the major findings on ADHD and executive functions and concluded: 50% of people with ADHD have deficits in executive functions although the deficits vary greatly by sort and kind. In addition, half of people with ADHD do not have any deficit in executive functions, therefore, it is impossible to rely only on tests that measure deficits in executive functioning when diagnosing ADHD. Moreover, it was found that difficulty in executive functions was more apparent in people with both ADHD and learning disorders. So it is legitimate to ask whether difficulty in executive functioning is more specific to learning disorders than it is to ADHD. Intelligence (IQ) also affects the relationship between ADHD and executive functioning (lower IQ relate also to lower executive functioning) and it is not clear which factor—IQ or ADHD—has the greater impact upon executive functioning (Seidman, 2006).

Since the data has been inconsistent and excessive heterogeneity characterize cognitive impairment in executive functions in people diagnosed with ADHD, another model has attempted to classify the various impairments in executive functions according to different types of ADHD (Sonuga-Barke, 2003). In this model, the deficits among people with ADHD can manifest either as "hot" or "cold" executive functions. Thus, people with ADHD can be classified according to "hot" or "cold" kinds of deficits in executive functioning.

"Cold" executive functions refer to response inhibition, planning, mental flexibility, switching strategies to obtain solutions, working memory, etc., which are the more common executive functions that have been analyzed in research on ADHD.

"Hot" executive functions refer to decision-making that is based upon emotions or motivation. Tests that measure "hot" executive functions ask respondents to choose between low-risk gambles with small potential for profit and high-risk gambles with potentially large profit or loss. Other tests compare instant receipt of small reinforcement with rejection of immediate satisfaction in order to receive subsequent large reinforcement. In support of this model, "hot" executive functions have been found to be associated with regions of the brain related to motivation and the processing of emotions while "cold" executive functions have not (Phan, Wagner, Taylor, & Liberzon, 2004).

However, studies on the relationship between ADHD and "cold" and "hot" executive functions have produced contradictory findings. On the one hand, children with ADHD were found to be low-functioning in both "cold" and "hot" executive functions even after controlling for comorbidities (Yang et al., 2011). On the other hand, children with ADHD and behavioral problems of Oppositional Defiant Disorder (ODD) were found to have lower capacity in "hot" executive functions than children with ADHD but without ODD (Humphreys & Lee, 2011). It has also been found that children with either ODD or delinquent behavior disorder show poor functioning in "hot" executive functions regardless of ADHD (Hobson, Scott, & Rubia, 2011). In addition, when comparing performance on tests that measure executive functions of both types, "cold" executive functions and "hot" executive functions among three groups of children aged 7-12, children with ADHD and ODD, children with ADHD but without ODD and children without these disorders (the control group), it was found that children with ADHD both with and without ODD showed lower functioning in "cold" executive functions, but not in "hot" executive functions. In addition, there were no significant differences between the two presentations (subtypes) of ADHD: ADHD inattentive without hyperactivity and ADHD with hyperactivity and impulsivity with respect to "hot" and "cold" executive functions (Antonini, Becker, Tamm, & Epstein, 2015; Skogli, Egeland, Andersen, Hovik, & Øie, 2014).

Thus, according to the literature, deficits in "hot" executive functioning seem to be related more to behavioral problems (ODD) than to ADHD. In addition, there is no difference between the two types of executive functions and the two subtypes of ADHD, so the distinction between "cold" and "hot" executive functions seems to be invalid for ADHD. Still, "cold" executive functioning appears to be impaired in people with ADHD but not consistently and without distinction between the presentations (subtypes) of ADHD.

Moreover, studies which examined the association of heredity to impairment in executive functioning found that while relatives with ADHD show impairment in executive functioning so do relatives without ADHD. Thus, although there is a genetic link to impairment in executive functioning, there is no direct link between these impairments and the behavioral symptoms of ADHD (Doyle, Biederman, Seidman, Reske-Nielsen, & Faraone, 2005).

Furthermore, although executive functions were found to be impaired in individuals with ADHD, impairment in executive functions are not exclusive to ADHD. In fact, impairment in executive functioning was found in children with dyslexia (reading disorder). These dyslectic children (without ADHD) showed significant difficulties in executive functioning relative to children without dyslexia and children with other learning difficulties in visual attention tests that measure executive functions (Lima, Azoni, Ciasca, 2011). In addition, children and adolescents who were diagnosed with major or secondary depression exhibited low functioning on tests which measure executive functions including working memory, executive attention and flexibility in decision-making (Holler, Kavanaugh, & Cook, 2014; McDermott, & Ebmeier, 2009). It has also been found that people with Obsessive-Compulsive Disorder (OCD) show dysfunction in executive functions, in particular in response inhibition, flexibility and change in strategy (Bédard, Joyala, Godbouta, & Chantal, 2009). In addition, one of the major disabilities in communication disorder in Autism Spectrum Disorder (ASD) is a deficiency in executive functioning (O'Hearn, Asato, Ordaz, & Luna, 2008). Moreover, findings suggest small but potentially meaningful associations between poverty and children's self-regulation (Hails, Zhou& Shaw, 2019). Furthermore, the common stimulant medications for the treatment of ADHD do not significantly improve the functioning of people with ADHD in tasks that measure executive functions (Seidman, 2006).

Thus, although one of the impairments in ADHD appears to be in executive functions, these impairments are not exclusive to or always present in the disorder. Thus, it cannot be argued that the behavioral symptoms of ADHD are exclusively related to impairment in executive functions.

ADHD and brain structures and functioning

As brain research has evolved over the past twenty years, many studies have focused on the relationship of ADHD to deficits in brain structure and functioning. People with ADHD were tested using electroencephalogram (EEG) brain scans and brain imaging - Magnetic Resonance Imaging (MRI) and Functional Magnetic Resonance Imaging (FMRI). MRI scans detect structural activity in a static mode while FMRI scans simulate dynamic activity when performing relevant tasks. The advantage of dynamic imaging is the possibility of focusing on dysfunction through some test and what it measures, but the disadvantage is that the conclusions are test-dependent and different tests have been associated to different brain activity. More recently developed measuring techniques such as Resting-State FMRI have produced more reliable results.

Usually low brain activity reflects low functioning. As a whole, results of brain-imaging show that children with ADHD have lower brain activity both in static conditions and when performing tests that theoretically measure response inhibition in some brain structures and their interactions, relative to children without ADHD. The main areas of low activity were the frontal areas (prefrontal cortex and inferior frontal gyrus), limbic system (anterior cingulate cortex), basal ganglia (striatum), cerebellum and the connections between these regions (Hart, Radua, Nakao, Mataix-Cols, & Rubia, 2013; Zhan, Liu, Wu, Gao, & Li, 2017). These are areas of the brain that are related to regulation, response-inhibition and motor planning. In distinction, in adults with ADHD, relative to children with ADHD, there appears to be inconsistency in the low activity registered in frontal areas which are considered responsible for response inhibition. According to some researchers, the difference between adults and children may be caused by the decrease in hyperactive and impulsivity symptoms in adults. Frontal regions continue to develop throughout adolescence, so physical development of these areas may produce the results indicative of higher functioning. The differences between adults with ADHD and children with ADHD may also be due to greater variation in the intensity of symptoms in adults and in the greater frequency of comorbidities such as depression in adults. These differences probably produce the differences in brain imaging (Banich, 2010).

However, no significant and consistent difference in brain activity was found between ADHD with presentations of inattention (without hyperactivity and impulsivity) and ADHD presentations with hyperactivity and impulsivity (Cortese et al., 2012; Ercan et al., 2016). This is not surprising since initially there was no significant difference between the two different presentations (subtypes) of ADHD in the cognitive neuropsychological tests that have often been used to detect dysfunctions in brain imagery (Willcuet et al., 2012). Another significant finding is that low activity in areas of the brain in people with ADHD, were dependent upon the severity of symptoms and IQ. It was found that children with severe ADHD and low IQ show significantly lower functioning and lower brain activity when compared to children with normal IQ and moderate ADHD and children without ADHD (Kyeong & Lee, 2016). Moreover, it was found that whenever ADHD was detected by means of advanced brain imaging, the diagnosis was relatively accurate. However, in a significant number of children who were diagnosed with ADHD using traditional clinical methods, the disorder was not detected by means of advanced brain imaging. These findings show that not everyone with ADHD has low brain activity and therefore, the disorder cannot be solely identified via diagnostic imaging (Oldehinkel, Francx, Beckmann, Buitelaar, & Mennes, 2013). It possible that only in severe cases of ADHD when low IQ is also present, low activity in relevant regions of the brain is also present and can therefore be detected by brain imaging.

In addition, different disorders such as communication disorder as in Autism Spectrum Disorder (ASD), Obsessive-Compulsive Disorder (OCD), bipolar disorder (manic depression) and other disorders have also show impaired activity in the same areas of the frontal and prefrontal cortexes, the limbic system (anterior cingulate cortex) and the basal ganglia (striatum) that are associated with ADHD. Thus, impaired activity in these areas is not exclusive to ADHD (Oldehinkel et al., 2013). Furthermore, low socioeconomic status was also found to be associated with reduced surface area in these regions. In these regions, environmentally mediated changes in the cerebellum and the caudate may be neuro-developmental mechanisms that explain the elevated risks of ADHD in children from families of low socioeconomic status (Machlin, McLaughlin, & Sheridan, 2020).

It is important to note that in FMRI imaging, brain activity was assessed using tests that theoretically measure response inhibition (for example, the go-no-go tests which are similar to the CPT) under the assumption that the main deficit in ADHD was response inhibition. As discussed above, this assumption is inaccurate. Both commission errors which are theoretically considered to measure response inhibition and omission errors which are associated with low arousal level and difficulties in sustained attention were evident and there was significant correlation between commission and omission errors. Therefore, it has been argued that low arousal and difficulties in sustained attention is the source of these errors (Avisar & Shalev, 2011; Johnson et al., 2007). The assumption that response inhibition is the major impairment in ADHD relates more to people with ADHD presentations of hyperactivity and impulsivity than to people with whose ADHD presentations center around inattentive behavior. Thus, these findings call into question the results and conclusions of brain imaging, since it is not clear if they actually measure impairment in response inhibition in ADHD at all.

Heredity and genetics

In recent years, the relation of heredity and genetics to ADHD has also been studied. Initially, the research sought to determine whether the disorder was inherited and if so, to what degree. The prevalence of the disorder in parents, siblings and twins in families with a child with ADHD was examined relative to families with an adopted child with ADHD. The findings show that parents who have a child with ADHD have two to eight times the likelihood of having ADHD and twin studies have shown that there is a 75% likelihood that ADHD is inherited (Faraone et al., 2005). According to these data, ADHD is one of the most hereditary psychiatric disorders.

In addition, studies have attempted to detect genes associated with the appearance of ADHD. These studies have focused on specific genes related to monoamine neurotransmitters and in particular, to the dopamine neurotransmitter. Dopamine is assumed to be associated with ADHD since low levels of dopamine in areas of the brain associated with symptoms of ADHD are prevalent. Stimulant medications for symptomatic treatment of ADHD such as Ritalin increase the amount of dopamine which in turn seems to reduce the symptoms.

Dopamine and serotonin transporter genes DAT1, DRD4, DRD5, 5HTT, SLC6A4, HTR1B were found to be weakly and inconsistently related to ADHD. The activity of these genes is also related to the heterogeneity of symptoms in ADHD as well as to symptoms of various other behavioral disorders.

Other studies did not focus on suspicious genes but did an overall scan of ADHD-related genes. These studies have identified genes CDH13, GFOD1 as possibly related to ADHD. However, the relations are weak and not exclusive as they were found to be related to other disorders as well. Hence, gene studies explain very little of the symptoms of ADHD.

Research has not reconciled the disparity between studies that show that ADHD is inherited with high prevalence (according to family and twin studies) and the weak findings of the gene studies that indicate that the relation between genetics and ADHD is inconclusive. The term "missing heritability" has been used to characterize this disparity. The first assumption about the disparity is that genetics is not sufficiently developed to find the significant correlations between specific genes and ADHD, although these correlations may exist. Another assumption states that ADHD is such a diverse disorder whose heterogeneous symptoms and numerous comorbidities present insurmountable difficulties in isolating the specific genes responsible for the various presentations (Salutino-Oliveira, Kieling, Rohde, & Hutz, 2013).

In some studies, a relation of low-to-moderate heredity has been found between ADHD and communication disorders (SCDC, ASD). Some studies have examined whether common genes are involved in these various disorders. Evidence has been found of a common genetic influence in ADHD and SCDC and ASD, although the effect is small and might be attributed to the heterogeneity of symptoms of ADHD and their changes over the course of a lifetime. Researchers have concluded that common genetic causes cannot be attributed to these disorders (Stergiakouli et al., 2017).

Environmental factors related to ADHD

Environmental factors including stroke, head injury, low birth weight, the mothers' prenatal smoking, exposure to lead and infection from streptococcus bacterium have also been found to relate to incidences of ADHD. In addition, psychological factors such as mothers' postpartum depression, a child's low socioeconomic status, life in an environment of low-stimulation, educational difficulties and difficulties in parenting were also found to be related to ADHD. Early exposure to stressful events is also known to affect regions of the brain associated with symptoms of ADHD (Humphreys et al., 2019; Machlin et al., 2020).

Extensive research on identical twins that examined the differences between them (the differences describes changes caused by the environment) found that approximately 40% of the symptoms of ADHD could be ascribed to environmental factors. The four-yearlong study did not distinguish between stable environmental factors and those that were circumstantial (Livingstone et al., 2016), but all the differences were attributed to environmental circumstances.

However, a significant number of environmental factors have been found to be mediators or enhancers of behavioral disorders and are sometimes related to comorbidities of ADHD, but they are not considered causal factors of ADHD (Greven, Asherton, Rijsdijk, & Plomin, 2011). furthermore, environmental influencers such as low birth weight which is related to the mother's smoking during pregnancy, her nutrition, depression and other factors have been linked to hypertension, diabetes, low intelligence, learning difficulties, anxiety disorders, depression and other health conditions (Nomura, 2007). These environmental factors were found to be related to ADHD but are not unique to the disorder. They have been related to ADHD's comorbidities. Thus, environmental factors are not sufficient to explain the etiology of ADHD.

Summary

In searching for the causes of ADHD, research initially focused on detecting neuropsychological impairment as the basis for the observed symptoms of ADHD. More recent studies have used brain imaging to detect specific brain structures and functions that are responsible for ADHD. Studies of heredity and genetics have attempted to find genes and environmental factors that cause or are related to ADHD.

Contrary to intuition and logic, selective mental attention function was found not to be a major deficit in ADHD. The fact that children with ADHD have no problems in playing video games demonstrates the notion that selective cognitive attention is not the main deficit in ADHD.

Disability in executive functions was found to only partially explain ADHD since a significant percentage of people with ADHD do not show deficits in executive functions. In addition, deficits in executive functions are not exclusive to ADHD and are related to intelligence, learning disabilities, communication disorders (e.g., ASD), depression, OCD and other disorders. Response inhibition which is as part of executive functions has been found to correlate to ADHD, but its relation to the inattentive (subtype) presentation that do not manifest hyperactivity and impulsivity symptoms of ADHD is unclear. Deficits in sustained attention/arousal show the most consistent relation to the behavioral symptoms of ADHD. Furthermore, people with ADHD consistently show poor functioning across all measures of sustained attention on Continuous Performance Tests (CPT). In addition, the stimulant medications used in treating ADHD show a positive influence upon performance on these tests. However, it should be noted that low-functioning on CPT tests has also been found in children with behavioral problems as Oppositional defiant disorder (ODD) who do not have ADHD. It was found that anxiety also affects performance on the CPT. Thus, it seems that deficiencies in sustained attention and response inhibition, as measured by CPT tasks, are not exclusive to ADHD.

Furthermore, no major mental neuropsychological deficit was found to differentiate between the behavioral symptoms of inattention versus impulsivity and hyperactivity and the different presentations (subtypes) of ADHD; ADHD inattentive vs. ADHD impulsivity and hyperactivity presentations. So, from a neuropsychological point of view, there is no theoretical justification for the different ADHD presentations (subtypes).

In addition, it is also important to note that there is no difference between boys and girls with ADHD in the performance of neuropsychological tasks (Seidman, 2006). Therefore, the findings with regard to ADHD are equally valid for both genders.

Because no unique neuropsychological dysfunction has been found to distinguish individuals with ADHD from individuals with other disorders, there is agreement that ADHD cannot be determined by neuropsychological tools alone. They can only be employed as diagnostic aids. As mentioned in Chapter 1, an acceptable diagnosis of ADHD can only be made by the examination behavioral symptoms of inattention, hyperactivity and impulsivity according to the DSM.

Imaging studies which examine the brain activity of people with ADHD have found that these individuals exhibit lower brain activity in the frontal and prefrontal regions, limbic system, basal ganglia, cerebellum and the pathways between them. These areas of the brain are responsible for attention, executive functioning, regulation, response inhibition and motor synchronization. Lower activity in these areas usually means lower functioning in these abilities.

However, lower brain activity in these areas appears to be more pronounced in children with severe ADHD and was also found to be related to low intelligence (IQ). Furthermore, studies of adults found inconsistent results regarding the relation between lower activity in these areas of the brain and ADHD. In addition, imaging studies have not detected a difference between the two different presentations of ADHD (ADHD inattentive without hyperactivity and impulsivity relative to ADHD with hyperactivity and impulsivity). Also, lower activity in areas of the brain found in people with ADHD were also seen in other disorders such as communication disorder, Autism Spectrum Disorder, Obsessive-Compulsive Disorder, and bipolar disorder (manic depression). Moreover, attempts to detect and diagnose ADHD via brain imaging alone were not successful since many children who were traditionally diagnosed with ADHD did not register low activity in brain scans. Thus, researchers concluded that brain imaging is not sensitive enough to serve as a diagnostic tool.

Consequently, despite great contributions in detecting impaired brain activity in structures and functions in ADHD, brain imaging has shown too much heterogeneity and inaccuracy in detecting ADHD. Thus, the findings on relations between brain activity and ADHD cannot be generalized to all people with ADHD. So even using brain imaging, an exclusive etiology for ADHD has not yet been found.

Studies on heredity and ADHD have shown that it is one of the most hereditary disorders. In addition, malfunction of several genes have been shown to increase the risk of inheriting the disorder. However, these genes were also found to be associated with other behavioral disorders. The difficulty in finding specific ADHD-related genes is attributed to the diversity and variability of the behavioral symptoms of ADHD as well as its various comorbidities. In addition, the divergence between the strong link to heredity in ADHD that was found in family studies and the weak link that so far has been found between specific genes and ADHD has caused researchers to name the phenomenon "missing heritability. "While the divergence may be due to heterogeneity and related difficulties of the disorder, exactly because of this, it is difficult to isolate genes and consolidate data which relate exclusively to this disorder.

As environmental factors found to be related to ADHD, are not unique to the disorder and probably relate more to its comorbidities, so environmental factors are deemed insufficient to explaining the etiology of ADHD.

Despite copious research, a specific, exclusive cause of ADHD has not yet been found, making the view that ADHD is a distinct disorder with specific and exclusive sources controversial (Lindstrøm, 2012). In addition, no differences were found in the sources or mediators of the inattention presentation of ADHD and the hyperactive and impulsive presentations of the disorder. While the division of the symptoms of ADHD into subtypes may be convenient for its relation to comorbidities and diagnosis according to the DSM, the etiologic validity of these different presentations does not seem to be justified (Willcuet et al., 2012).

Chapter 4

Treatment of ADHD

There are several main treatments for ADHD:

The drug treatment
- Intended for treatment of symptoms of inattention and lack of concentration and for reducing symptoms of hyperactivity and impulsivity

Non-drug treatments
- Behavioral treatments employing behavioral management and parental guidance. Intended to improve self-control and capabilities for restraint in people with ADHD who also have behavioral difficulties
- Educational programs and interventions in schools and in classroom settings. Similar to behavioral management, it is intended to improve collaboration and functioning in school

- Recommendations for environmental adaptations and learning approaches that are tailored to the difficulties encountered
- Therapeutic intervention to improve social management. The focus is on social skills which include self-awareness, improvements to elicit positive social interactions, understanding of the Other and the Other's needs, interpersonal communication and collaboration.
- Therapeutic approaches that elevate awareness and self-control such as: mindfulness, biofeedback, etc.
- Most importantly, fostering of constructive attitudes that promote and emphasize strengths over disabilities in order to elevate self-esteem, self-efficacy and motivation.

Drug treatment for ADHD

Drug treatment is the most common "remedy" for ADHD. Drug therapy does not "cure" but rather reduces symptoms under the active influence of the medication. When the effect of the medication expires, the situation is back to where it was.

While a variety of medications exist, the most common and the most effective are the ones best known by their trade names: Ritalin, Ritalin LA, Ritalin SR, Concerta, Daytrana, and Focalin and belong to the category of stimulants whose active ingredient is methylphenidate. The difference among them is in their mode of operation and the duration of the effect, both of which are related to the drugs' side-effects. The duration of the effect of Ritalin is four hours with a relatively pronounced influence at the onset and a steep decrease in effect after four hours. Ritalin is considered to have more side-effects than Concerta since the potency of Concerta lasts up to twelve hours with a relatively modest decrease in effect after twelve hours.

However, it is important to mention that side-effects are a matter of individual experience. Hence, the dosage of each specific drug needs to be adjusted to every individual user.

These drugs have a psychoactive effect on the central nervous system. They elevate the level of the neurotransmitter dopamine in the brain and probably also elevate the level of the neurotransmitters serotonin and norepinephrine (which is also called noradrenaline). This is done by pre-synaptic stimulation which releases dopamine and blocks its reuptake.

In addition, there are stimulant medications whose active substance is amphetamine elevate the level of dopamine in a manner similar to that of the methylphenidates. However, this is accomplished by greater pre-synaptic stimulation then Methylphenidate but without blocking reuptake. The trade names of amphetamine-containing stimulants are: Adderall, Attent, and Vyvanse.

Common side-effects of these stimulant medications are loss of appetite (In the 1980 these stimulants also served as diet pills for weight loss), headaches, nausea (although this is more common at the beginning of treatment) and sleep disorders, because of which it is not recommended to take these medications in the evening. These drugs can also affect children's height and weight (Huang & Tsai, 2011). In addition, the presentation of or the worsening of tics (involuntary movements such as eye blinking) and the elevation of Tourette's Syndrome (motor and vocal tics such as sniffing and beeping) have also been reported. With the appearance of tics or a family history of Tourette's Syndrome, hypertension or epilepsy, caution must be taken when prescribing a specific drug treatment.

Research on animals has shown that high doses of stimulant drugs can cause hypertension, impaired cardiovascular functioning and damage to the central nervous system. In studies of humans there are rare reports of psychotic states and hallucinations upon exposure to high doses of these medications. However, it is important to note that significantly higher doses of these stimulants have been used in animal research relative to the doses used for people with ADHD. So, risk of damage is small.

Other side-effects of these stimulant medications sometimes occur when the effect of the drug wears off. A rebound effect sometimes manifests as temporary worsening of the symptoms of ADHD. To avoid this, physicians recommend adding low dosages of the medication at the end of the initial dose or alternatively using a stimulant medication with a slow-release mechanism (Santosh & Taylor, 2000).

It has also been found that both among people with anxiety and people with ADHD and co-morbidities of anxiety, stimulant medications can aggravate that anxiety or its side-effects (Buitelaar, Van der Gaag, Swaab-Barneveld & Kuiper, 1995; Pliszka, 1989). This may be due to the fact that anxiety is characterized by over-arousal and over-activation and stimulant drugs which increase arousal just may cause over-arousal, aggravating the initial anxiety even further.

One of the common myths concerning the stimulants used in the treatment of ADHD is that they only improve the ability to concentrate in those with ADHD. This is not accurate! In fact, already in World War II, soldiers who served as nighttime controllers in command positions used these drugs to maintain alertness. Many citizens in Germany during the War were also taken to function better. Stimulants whose active ingredient is the same as that used in the treatment of ADHD have been found to improve athletic performance and to facilitate recovery after an injury. *The World Anti-Doping Association (WADA) defines these drugs as "prohibited for competitive use." Hence, an athlete may be penalized or prevented from competing for a number of years if he or she has used stimulants unless under special permission for medical purposes (Wienersky, 2018).*

Furthermore, many people who do not have ADHD use these drugs to maintain alertness and concentration and to function better at work (Rasmussen, 2008). The use of stimulants is very common among students in the US and Canada (Poulin, 2007; Smith and Farah, 2011). A survey conducted in Israel found that many students use illegally obtained stimulant medications to achieve better exam results (Kellner, 2013). In addition, stimulants can also improve concentration in children without ADHD (Rapoport et al., 1980). Moreover, there are children with ADHD for whom stimulant medication therapy does not significantly improve functioning. In light of the above, it is important to note that the effect of drug therapy is not reliable and, therefore, consideration of its impact is unacceptable when diagnosing ADHD.

Other medications for ADHD that do not belong to the stimulant category are generally less effective and are usually given when stimulant medication does not work or is accompanied by too many side-effects. For example, a drug known by the trade name of "Strattera" contains atomoxetine which inhibits reuptake of norepinephrine in the synaptic intervals in the brain, which is derived from Adrenaline (Norepinephrine Reuptake Inhibitor; NRI) thereby elevating its concentration. Unlike stimulant medications, the effect of Straterra is not instantaneous and is felt only after a week at least. This drug was initially used as a treatment for depression and anxiety but was subsequently found to improve attention. While these medications are less effective for ADHD relative to stimulant medications, their effect is constant throughout the day. The side-effects are different from those of stimulants so for those with ADHD who are debilitated by the side-effects of stimulants, treatment with Straterra can be a better solution. In addition, due to its efficacy in treating depression and anxiety, it can be effective for people with ADHD who also have these emotional co-morbidities.

How stimulant drug treatment reduces symptoms of ADHD

Before reviewing the findings on the action of stimulant drug treatments in ADHD, it is important to note that intuition suggests that stimulants should increase hyperactivity. Paradoxically these medications actually reduce hyperactivity while increasing the ability to concentrate. It turns out that stimulant medications reduce the symptoms of all subtypes of ADHD. They are equally effective for people with presentations of inattention (without hyperactivity and impulsivity) as they are for people with presentations of hyperactivity and impulsivity (Wang et al., 2011).

How stimulant medications operate on people with ADHD is not fully understood. However, one theory is that people with ADHD lack sufficient amounts of the neurotransmitter dopamine in the frontal and prefrontal regions of the brain. This deficiency leads to low neural activity in these areas which are responsible for regulating and inhibiting response. The elevation of dopamine levels obtained by the use of stimulant medications increases neural activity in these areas, improving the ability to self-regulate and inhibit responses, which in turn reduces the symptoms of hyperactivity and impulsivity in those with ADHD (Rubia, Alegria, & Brinson, 2014). However, this theory does not explain why stimulant medications are so efficacious in improving attention, concentration and functioning in people whose ADHD presentation is inattentiveness without hyperactivity and impulsivity. Exactly how do stimulants improve the functioning of those with ADHD whose difficulty is not response inhibition?

Another theory states that stimulant medications increase the intrinsic level of arousal and thus increase alertness. This in turn reduces the need for external stimulation which improves attention and reduces hyperactivity. According to this theory, people with ADHD who lack alertness look for external stimulation to raise their alertness and this leads to Difficulties in focus and maintain on specific stimulus. This is the cause of low concentration and hyperactivity and is consistent with the claim that the neuropsychological basis for the symptoms of ADHD is low arousal (Douglas, 1972). It posits a similarity between low arousal and fatigue which also decreases concentration and the ability to plan and increases impatience and impulsivity. In infants, fatigue is often characterized by nervousness and hyperactivity.

The fact that stimulant medications generate arousal gives support to this theory. Accordingly, findings have shown that stimulant medications influence wide areas of the brain that are susceptible to arousal and not just the frontal regions (Rubia et al., 2014). The greatest efficacy of stimulant medications in cases of ADHD is found in the improved results on cognitive CPT tests which measure arousal and sustained attention. Hence, early versions of these tests were called Vigilance CPT. However, the efficacy of these drugs in tests of executive functioning is inconsistent and questionable (Gardner, Sheppard, & Efron, 2008; Pietrzak, Mollica, Maruff, & Snyder, 2006; Riccio, Waldrop, Reynolds, & Lowe, 2001). In practice, the effectiveness of stimulant medication therapy is ascertained by CPT tests. In the recent past the Test of Variable Attention (TOVA) was also used for examining the efficiency of stimulants. Although it is important to note that stimulant medications increase functioning in newer versions of CPT tasks that also measure response inhibition. However, there is still some doubt that the CPT response inhibition measure is not actually the result of arousal and sustained attention functions (Johnson et al., 2007).

The efficacy of the drug treatment for ADHD
Over the past fifty years, Ritalin and other stimulant medications have been the most prescribed treatment for

children with ADHD and since the 1990s use of stimulants has increased by hundreds of percentage points (Holden et al., 2013). Many studies show that these medications are effective in reducing symptoms of inattention, hyperactivity and impulsivity in people with ADHD in the short-term. In addition, drug treatment leads to a significant improvement in learning and social and emotional functioning (Evans & Pelham, 2001; Santosh & Taylor, 2000; Swanson, Baler & Volkow, 2011). Stimulant medications have been shown to reduce aggression and behavioral problems, improve relationships between children and parents and between children and authority figures as well as improve children's relationships with friends and peers (Wolraich, 2003).

Studies investigating the effect of stimulant medications on functioning show that the most positive response to stimulant medications occurs among those with ADHD who exhibit high hyperactivity, severe attention deficits and minor emotional disorders (Overmeyer & Taylor, 1999). On the other hand, children with ADHD and learning disorders respond less favorably to stimulant therapy than do children with ADHD but with no learning disorders as stimulants do not significantly improve learning disorders (Gittelman, Klein & Feingold, 1983; Grizenko, Bhat, Schwartz, Ter-Stepanian & Joober, 2006).

In the long- term, there is less consensus regarding improvement in performance on learning tasks due to stimulant medication therapy (Santosh & Taylor, 2000). Accordingly, it was found that children with ADHD who received long-term stimulant drug treatment continued to show the same difficulty in learning at the end of elementary school as they did at the beginning (van der Schans et al., 2017). This was also true of the long-term improvement in accomplishing learning tasks among high school children with ADHD who received drug treatments (Powers, Marks, Miller, Newcorn, & Halperin, 2008).

The findings on the efficacy of stimulant drugs have primarily relied on reports from parents, teachers or professionals, with only a few studies based on reports from the children and adolescents who received the drug treatment. Studies based on both child and parental reports found that improvement in educational functioning was the parents' main benefit while the child-based reports mainly centered on the treatment "price". side-effects which included feelings of disconnection, changes in personality and lack of motivation to participate in social activities (Efron, Jarman, & Barker, 1998; Harpur, Thompson, Daley, Abikoff & Sonuga-Barke, 2008; McNeal, Roberts, & Barone, 2000). Accordingly, children reported less improvement and sometimes even a worsening in their quality-of-life especially in the social domain as a result of taking stimulant medications (Coghill, 2010). Furthermore, one study that interviewed students with ADHD about their experiences with drug therapy from childhood to the present reported that most respondents related unpleasant childhood experiences under the influence of stimulant medications, such as a feeling of disconnection and apathy, a sense of a change in identity, generalized lethargy and lack of desire to work. Some students said that the stimulant medications made it difficult for them to interact socially because they felt disconnected– as if they were in a bubble– and thus the drug impaired their social ability (Meaux, Hester, Smith, & Shoptaw, 2006).

In another study, adolescents with ADHD who discussed their long-term experiences with stimulant medication therapy said that they had to deal with abdominal pain, loss of appetite, fatigue, a change in identity, a decrease in mood and a lack of desire for social participation. About half of the adolescents said that drug treatment did not help them in school because the headaches and fatigue that accompanied the treatment impaired their functioning. Almost everyone reported that drug treatment increased their short-term ability to concentrate but the persistent side-effects and the decreased motivation to participate in social activities created a desire to discontinue the drug treatment. In childhood, they had difficulty convincing their parents to stop administering the drugs. However, by junior high school, most of the adolescents significantly reduced the drug treatment on their own (Avisar, 2014; Avisar & Lavie-Ajayi, 2014). This is consistent with the literature which reports a significant decrease in use of the drug treatment as children become adolescents (Price, Ford, Janssens, Williams, & Newlove-Delgado, 2020) since this is the period when dependence upon parents wanes. Adolescents reported that they took the drug treatment in childhood in compliance with the wishes of adults and not necessarily in accordance with their own wishes (Harpur et al., 2008; Meauxet et al., 2006). However, some adolescents reported that they continued to selectively take stimulant medications during tests, benefiting from improved concentration and better functioning without having to pay the price of the side-effects that accompany a daily drug treatment regimen (Avisar & Lavie-Ajayi, 2014). Although it is important to note that, only a small proportion of adolescents who stopped ADHD medication subsequently resumed their prescriptions in primary care (Newlove-Delgado, Ford, Hamilton, Janssens, & Stein, 2019).

Non-drug treatments for ADHD

While drug treatment is the most common treatment for ADHD, it has some disadvantages as has been shown. Reduction of short-term behavioral symptoms of ADHD is compensated by the return of symptoms– sometimes with greater intensity–when its effect expires. Then coping with the difficulties– mostly within the family framework– sometimes causes clashes between the child with ADHD and his/her siblings and parents. In addition, although drug treatments increase functionality which results in better behavior, the impact on long-term academic achievement is in dispute. Moreover, side-effects such as abdominal pain, loss of appetite, change in identity, and sleep disorders cause discomfort and restlessness and impact the daily discipline of taking the medications.

Most importantly, drug treatment doesn't "cure", and long-term drug treatment doesn't promote coping skills for dealing with the core symptoms of the disorder (Daly, Creed, Xanthopoulos & Brown, 2007). Hence, some interventions combine drug treatment with other non-drug interventions in order to obtain greater effect for the long term.

Non-drug treatments primarily focus on the ability to cope with the consequences of the disorder. On a practical level, these treatments focus on behavioral difficulties and behavioral change. Most of these treatments do not readjust the symptoms of inattention or hyperactivity but aim at changing the expression of the disorder and reducing behavioral and functional problems over time.

Behavior Management Therapy

Behavior Management Therapy, the oldest method that has been developed can achieve long-term results if implemented correctly (Lundahl, Risser, & Lovejoy, 2006). Significant parental guidance is required in order to obtain long-lasting results. Behavioral Management primarily focuses on the child's behavioral problems with his or her parents as initial authority figures. As a rule, the younger the child the greater the dependence upon parents and the more interaction there is between them. And therefore, a more parental guidance is needed for more effecting results. The general assumption is that an improved relationship between the child and the parents will be generalized and its impact felt in interactions with other authority figures.

Treatment begins with an analysis of the causes and goals of the unwanted behaviors (for example: the goal of gaining attention as secondary reinforcement since parents relate to and pay attention to the child only when he/she behaves improperly). The idea is to deal with unwanted behavior in ways that ultimately reduce it. For example, ignoring the child so that he/she does not get the desired attention as a secondary reinforcement.

Most importantly, the second crucial phase of the treatment is to analyze the praise and awards that the child desires and is affected by and that will serve as reinforcements for instilling proper behavior, for example, paying more attention when the child behaves properly. The idea is to reinforce positive activities such as bicycle-riding or surfing and to praise positive actions. Sports are often a good reinforcement for hyperactive children. Sometimes problems arise when parents who are not fond of outdoor activity expect a hyperactive child to sit still. When the child has difficulty complying, it can lead to rebuke, criticism, secondary reinforcement of attention for improper behavior, continuous conflict and escalation of negative feelings in the child-parent relationship. The goal of Behavior Management Therapy is to break this vicious cycle and to find a way to alter it the positive direction.

Behavior Management Therapy can be applied through a regimen wherein the child earns points toward a desired prize by learning ways to resolve conflict, restrain negative behavior and get help from adults. In order to succeed, the focus first is on minor disruptive behavior that parents deem is important to correct and that they can handle. Parents need to "choose their battles." Penalties and reinforcements should be individually customized to each child according to his/her age.

It is important to persevere with the regimen in order to bring about a change in behavior. While the theory is simple, the practice is difficult. Failure is most often due to the inability to maintain the program over time. It can be reasonably said that not only the child, but also the adult has to change in order for the program to succeed.

As mentioned, the aim of Behavioral management therapy is to reduce behavioral problems associated with ADHD and not the core symptoms of inattention and hyperactive which are less changeable. The Behavioral Management paradigm is appropriate for all children with behavior problems not only those who do not have ADHD.

Education programs and interventions in school and in classroom settings

Therapeutic interventions in the classroom are long-standing, highly effective and widely used (DuPaul & Eckert, 1997). In principle, the intervention is similar to that of Behavior Management Therapy and focuses on reducing unwanted classroom behavior and reinforcing appropriate behavior. In the initial stage, the most disruptive behaviors are analyzed, their causes are hypothesized, and appropriate reinforcements are designed. This analysis is done in consultation with every child with ADHD so that they agree to reducing certain behaviors and approve of the reinforcements that will be used.

Methods to execute the program include accumulating points for avoiding disruptive behavior while accumulating points for proper behavior. Sometimes a chart of accumulated points is applied to all children in the class. Cards of selected behaviors are displayed, and a child's behavior is reported to that child's parents. In applying the program to older children and adolescents, a contract can be drawn up with behaviors that the child undertakes to improve balanced against appropriate sets of rewards.

In order to maintain the uniformity of messages from both teacher and parents, parental cooperation with the program is important. Similar to Behavioral Management Therapy, commitment and perseverance on the part of teachers and parents are necessary in order for these programs to be effective.

Therapeutic intervention to improve academic achievement

Since children with ADHD have difficulty maintaining attention, difficulty in sitting still and difficulty in practicing patience, they often have difficulty learning. This in turn affects academic achievement. Focused learning programs employing close instruction with computer-assisted instruction that conveys specific topics helps raise awareness and increase motivation. These techniques have been found to contribute to higher functioning and higher academic achievement. In addition, learning strategies that include briefing, organization of materials, organizing aids, dividing the material to be learned into small modules, providing time for refreshment with breaks to restore concentration and teaching strategies for reading comprehension have been found to be effective (Zentall & Leib, 1985). Furthermore, adjustment in methods of evaluation and testing such as enabling oral presentations for those who have difficulty organizing and expressing themselves in writing have also been found to be effective in enabling students to express knowledge and increase achievement (Dubey & O'Leary, 1975).

It is important to note that Behavior Management Therapy also contributes to academic achievement and therefore integration of behavioral management into the learning methods described above increases efficiency. When building a program, it is important to note that every child with ADHD has different abilities and different learning styles, so understanding and using the strengths of that child's learning ability can contribute to increased motivation and achievement.

Therapeutic interventions to improve social interaction

People with ADHD and especially those who present hyperactive and impulsive symptoms often show difficulties in social situations. Impulsive unregulated reactions like outbursts of anger, arguments, bullying or aggression are prone to occur. In addition, it was found that people with ADHD are often unaware of this aspect of their personalities and do not feel that their unregulated behavior is detrimental to their social interactions (Hoza et al., 2000).

Since, social difficulty has been found to be one of the most significant causes of long-term emotional, medical, and functional problems (Rubin, Bukowski & Parker, 1998), it is important to improve social interaction skills in children with ADHD and in children that have social difficulties in general. Although drug treatment is effective in reducing negative behavior, it does not promote positive behavior and does not contribute significantly to the social status of children with ADHD (Landau & Moore, 1991). Therefore, therapeutic interventions that improve social skills like seem to be very important.

Therapeutic interventions which seek to improve social interactions focuses on social skills that include: improving self-awareness of pro-social behavior, understanding the Other and the Other's needs, interpersonal communication and collaboration are beneficial. These interventions are done in small therapeutic groups organized around analyzing social interactions and developing social skills in a controlled environment. The idea behind it is that the social skills acquired in the therapeutic group will be generalized to everyday social interactions. Social skill and social awareness can also be fostered through classroom activities with the mediation of teachers and parents and with the guidance of psychologists. The advantage of using the classroom setting is that relevant situations and interactions can be analyzed in a real peer group.

Studies examining the effectiveness of acquiring social skill via group interventions alone have found that improvement is incomplete or insufficient for enhancement of the social status of children with ADHD especially those whose ability to maintain social relations is limited. In order to achieve significant improvement, it was necessary to intervene with all children in the classroom to make them understand, accept and share the experience of social rejection of the disadvantaged children. It was also found that intervention to enhance social skill together with individual interventions using Behavioral Management Therapy under parental cooperation significantly improved the social status of the children with ADHD (Frankel, Myatt, Cantwell & Feinberg, 1997).

Furthermore, researchers maintain that in order to improve long-term social interaction, therapeutic interventions should encourage the formation of a close friendship over time is needed. Accordingly, interventions that pair a child with ADHD who is experiencing social difficulty with a suitable child who does not have ADHD (taking into consideration parental consent, preferences, adjustments, etc.) have been developed. In order for the intervention to be effective, parents must be persistent in initiating meet-ups that have positive and interesting activities that the two children want to engage in so as to encourage and increase the motivation and desire for additional meet-ups. This can be challenging because it depends on the wishes of another parent and child. However, when such interventions have succeeded, the friendships formed have been found to improve long-term social development of children with ADHD who have social difficulties (Hoza, Mrug, Pelham, Greiner, & Gnagy, 2003).

Therapeutic approaches that elevate awareness and self-control

There are some methods that promote awareness of emotional and behavioral regulation have been developed. These methods developed for various disorders and not specifically for ADHD. However, these methods may also help people with ADHD to better control and regulate their emotions and their behavior.

Mindfulness, the psychological process of purposely bringing one's attention to experiences occurring at the present moment without judging them is one such example. Mindfulness can be cultivated through meditation and other practices. It stands to reason that any form of attention-training that hones self-control would be a remedy for ADHD.

A number of studies highlight the possible benefits of mindfulness-based therapies in reducing the symptoms of children with ADHD (Cairncross & Miller, 2016). Most studies of adults showed improvement of ADHD symptoms. Moreover, that training in mindfulness and meditation improves some aspects of executive functioning and emotion dysregulation. However, the relatively low criteria for selection and performance in several of the studies calls for caution in interpreting the results (Poissant, Mendrek, Talbot, Khoury, & Nolan, 2019).

Biofeedback (neurofeedback) is another method for gaining greater awareness of physiological functions. It uses instrumentation to provide information on the activity of neurologic systems with the ultimate goal of being able to manipulate them at will. This paradigm may have potential for controlling the attention deficits and the impulsivity that characterize ADHD. So far, the research on the effectiveness of neurofeedback for those with ADHD is inconclusive. While some scientists have found it to be only "possibly helpful," for ADHD. other studies on children have shown a medium reduction of symptoms of ADHD that lasts for up to six months, following treatment (Van et al., 2019).

Cognitive Behavioral Therapy (CBT) is a psychological treatment approach that focuses on challenging and changing unhelpful cognitive distortions – thoughts, beliefs, and attitudes– and in so doing improves emotional regulation and aids in developing coping strategies that address current problems. Thus, CBT is used for several psychological disorders and may help people with ADHD develop a more planned and reflective approach especially in social interactions. A meta-analysis of CBT in adults with ADHD showed CBT had small-to-medium effect on self-reported symptoms and functioning versus controls (Knouse, Teller, & Brooks, 2017).A study on the use of CBT in children with ADHD found that parental perception of their children's hyperactivity in the home indicated a decrease in these activities and that child-rated self-esteem improved when compared to a control group using a different supportive therapy (Fehlings, 1991).

While the above-mentioned therapies may be beneficial for people with ADHD. It's not entirely reasonable that short-term interventions can improve its core symptoms, since ADHD consider a neurodevelopmental disorder. It is possible, however, that these interventions may improve the ability to control or bypass the difficulties encountered by developing other abilities which improves the coping skills. Hence, the overall functioning of people with ADHD improves. It should also consider that every person is different and Since there usually is no pure disorder without accompanying difficulties, these methods that indirectly improve functioning may ultimately improve the quality of life of people with ADHD. In addition, it seems that adults benefit more than children from some of these interventions, perhaps because adults have more interest in developing the self-awareness that allows them to control their lives. Although these therapies have no cost (other than possibly financial), they are not considered to be the first-line treatment for ADHD and should be considered as such.

Constructive attitudes that promote and emphasize strengths rather than disabilities

Some researchers do not view ADHD as a disorder at all and suggest that ADHD is a unique temperament found at the end of the normal personality range. (reminiscent of the energy temperament which attribute to redheads). Accordingly, the most prominent personality traits of ADHD are disorganization, restlessness and extroversion (which relate more to the hyperactive presentation of ADHD), creativity, openness to experience (found in children with ADHD who have high intelligence) and sensation-seeking (Nigg et al., 2002; White, 1999). Although this approach clashes with the medical approach that considers exception as abnormality, it allows for a different therapeutic view. Hence, instead of trying to reduce the symptoms of ADHD, which is not really possible except through constant drugging, the idea is to encourage the person with ADHD to develop his or her strengths and motivations and to channel them toward a positive outcome. While at the same time reducing the pressure to eliminate his or her weaknesses. In other words, the aim is to strengthen self-esteem, self-confidence and belief in one's own ability to achieve success, instead of causing overwhelming frustration and a sense of failure by trying to eliminate behavioral difficulties.

For example, instead of scolding a hyperactive child for not sitting still, allow the child to participate in sports where hyperactivity is an advantage. Accordingly, studies have found that when focusing on long-term health benefits in children and adolescents with ADHD, qualitative exercise may play an important role (Neudecker, Mewes, Reimers & Woll, 2019). Also, not directing unorganized people into areas of learning that require strict order such as bookkeeping but rather toward acting, art or some other creative activity where their imaginations can be freely expressed.

In this context, it is interesting to note that the Israeli army's extensive research on ADHD convinced them to change their approach. Candidates with ADHD were evaluated and except for a remark in the Learning Disorder section, that person's medical profile (A medical profile is the competence score of every soldier) was not lowered because of ADHD. Consequently, soldiers with ADHD were allowed to serve in combat units, commando units and the infantry. They were able to advance in the military hierarchy, according to their level of functioning and their dependence upon drug treatments and were entitled to become officers (Achikam, 2013). The military understood that contrary to the myth, the cognitive ability to ignore stimuli is not impaired in people with ADHD especially in non-standard environments and environments that do not require long periods of sitting as occurs in school. Soldiers with ADHD had no difficulty in functioning in a demanding, multi-stimuli setting. Soldiers and officers with ADHD in the Israeli army are flourishing and fulfilling themselves perhaps because of − and not in spite of − their hyperactivity and their need for excitement and a multitude of stimuli.

Many professional athletes at the highest level also have ADHD. In addition, and probably for the same benefits of the disorder, their incidence is about twice as high in sport team and individual sports as it is in the general population. A few examples of outstanding athletes who have ADHD diagnoses are Michael Phelps who won eight Olympic medals in swimming, Simon Bayles, who won several Olympic gold medals in gymnastics, Michael Jordan, the legendary basketball player, the sprinter Justin Gatlin, the gymnast Lewis Smith and water-jump star Mogger Lognis, football star Terry Bradshaw and baseball star Pete Rose. It is important to note that most of these athletes were not on medication either because there was no need or because stimulant medications are illegal in competitive sports and require special permission. Some of these athletes did take stimulant medications in their childhood, perhaps to overcome learning difficulties in the education system (Weinerski, 2018). As mentioned, in challenging environments where it is necessary to respond quickly, be focused and avoid distraction, these athletes did not have difficulty managing attention. It even appears that their ability to do so is greater than most normal people, which refutes a number of myths about ADHD.

It appears that the ADHD temperament is also an advantage in acting. Israel has several leading actors who have been diagnosed with ADHD (due to individual confidentiality, their names are not specified here) and who were able to channel their abundant energy into high-level performances on stage.

The evidence presented here shows that a good deal of treatment and therapeutic interventions for ADHD should focus on individual strengths as opposed to an excess emphasis on treating the difficulties inherent to the disorder. Activities in which having ADHD is an advantage can lead to personal success and this in turn can be a springboard for constructive and healthy development. Hence, participation in these activities should be encouraged.

Summary

Stimulant medications like Ritalin and other methylphenidate compounds have been the most common treatment for ADHD for over fifty years. Over the past twenty years Over the last twenty years their use has increased by hundreds of percentage points. Stimulant medications have significantly reduced the behavioral symptoms of inattention, hyperactivity and impulsivity in people with ADHD in the short-term. In addition, these stimulants medications have also produced better learning outcomes, a reduction in behavioral problems, improvement in interpersonal interactions and improvement in accepting authority.

However, the long-term effectiveness of these medications in boosting learning outcomes has been questioned. Moreover, stimulant medications have been found to be less effective for children with ADHD and learning disorders relative to children with ADHD and no learning disorders. This is because stimulant medications do not "cure", but only provide immediate relief of the behavioral symptoms of ADHD, but do not address learning disorders or the educational or emotional difficulties that are not a direct result of ADHD.

Drug therapy has side-effects that include physical discomfort (nausea and headaches (which decrease over time), feelings of a change in identity, and lack of desire to participate in social interactions. These have been widely reported by children who have received stimulant medications treatment. Moreover, studies have shown that in transitioning to adolescence and from elementary school to junior high school, a significant decline in daily use of stimulant medication occurs, mainly due to adolescents'' asserting their own preference not to take the drug (decrease in parental dependence that allows adolescents to reduce the medications consumption). Although, in high school, some adolescents with ADHD selectively took stimulant medications when studying for tests or to perform better on the tests themselves. In so doing, they said that they benefited from the improvement in concentration while avoiding the side-effects associated with regular use of the medications.

One of the common myths concerning stimulant medications is that they are only effective for ADHD. But in fact, as early as World War II, the drug was given to soldiers in command positions, combat soldiers and citizens to raise their concentration, alertness and functioning. In addition, many students and adults without ADHD have used stimulant medications to improve their functioning. They have been found effective in improving focus in learning environments and in work environments requiring concentration even though those who used them did not have ADHD. Therefore, stimulant use is not a diagnostic for ADHD, so the disorder cannot be diagnosed by the effect of the medication: In other words, a positive effect is not an indication of ADHD nor is the absence of an effect a negation of the existence of ADHD.

It is important to note that although stimulant medications are highly effective in increasing focus and concentration and reduce hyperactivity and impulsivity. But in cases of disorders involving anxiety or a co-morbidity of anxiety and ADHD, there is a high possibility that the condition may worsen, and anxiety may actually increase. If people with this condition do not respond favorably to first-line stimulant medications, there are alternative non-stimulant drugs that can be used although their efficacy to improve concentration is lower than that of the stimulants. these non-stimulant medications are also a good solution for other emotional and mental disorders co-morbidities.

While drug treatment is the most common therapy, non-drug treatments for ADHD are also available. These non-drug treatment interventions focus on Behavioral Management Therapy for reducing behavioral problems in children with ADHD who exhibit behavioral problems. Behavior management therapy administered by the parents of the child with ADHD, accompanied by parental guidance. As a rule, the younger the child, the more effective Behavioral Management Therapy is as the child is more dependent upon his/her parents. The theory behind Behavior management therapy emphasizes non-reinforcement of unwanted behavior; for example, by not providing attention (as a secondary benefit) in situations of impaired behavior and not prolonging conflicts. The operative principle is that children earn points or gain prizes and praise either for good behavior or for avoiding unwanted behavior.

Similarly, in the classroom, behavioral management programs undertaken by teachers are particularly effective if done in conjunction with feedback and in collaboration with the child's parents. For learning problems, use of teaching strategies that employ briefing, organizing the material, organizing aids, learning in small modules, allocation of time for refreshment and breaks, working with stimulating computer programs along with adjustments in tests that include writing assistance or oral tests for those with ADHD who have difficulty in expressing themselves in writing have been found to be effective. This combination of strategies has been shown to boost long-term achievement.

Another therapeutic intervention involves improving social skills by raising awareness of mutuality and better communication with friends and peer groups. Therapeutic interventions that encourage the formation of a close friendship over time are also effective. This can be achieved through small and intimate group therapy with an emphasis on social skills, sports or active involvement of the child's parents.

The advantages of non-drug treatment over drug treatment is that: while drug treatment relieves the short-term symptoms of inattention, hyperactivity and impulsivity, it doesn't cure or brings about better ability to cope with the long-term consequences of the disorder. The drug treatment also has side effects which are sometimes hard to deal. In contrast, the non-drug treatments have none of the deleterious side-effects of drug treatments so in the long-run they focus on improving the ability to cope with the consequences of the disorder for produce a healthier and more satisfying quality-of-life. It should be noted that non-drug treatment requires more effort and persistence over time. Thus, researchers have found that the best results are achieved by combining both approaches. To the extent that drug treatment reduces ADHD's core symptoms of inattention, hyperactivity and impulsivity in the short-term, it enables more availability for non-drug treatments to effect long-term behavioral improvements. In any case, the advice for the long-term is not to renounce non-drug therapies.

It is important to note the uniqueness of every person who diagnosed with ADHD. No two cases are alike. This extends to both the two presentations (subtypes) of ADHD (with or without hyperactivity and impulsivity) that are express differently and the cases of ADHD with co-morbidities that present different emotional, behavioral and social problems. Usually, instances of ADHD with hyperactivity and impulsivity presentations exhibit more behavioral and social difficulties than those with just attention deficits. In addition, regardless of the different presentations of ADHD, there are differences in learning ability, learning difficulties and disorders, co-morbidities and the severity of ADHD manifest as different functional impairments. In light of the fact that each person with ADHD has their own unique mental structure and motivation, these need to be taken into account when choosing the appropriate treatment. For example, a child who does not have behavioral difficulties does not need to undergo in Behavioral Management Therapy intervention. A child with ADHD and a learning disorder will probably benefit more from learning adjustments than from medication.

It is essential to constantly verify the effectiveness of any treatment with the child. Overall quality-of-life as measured on emotional, social, and behavioral scales must be considered and not only achievement in the educational domain. Treatments that do not meet these criteria must be changed.

Moreover, some researchers do not view ADHD as a disorder at all and suggest that the condition is just a unique temperament at the end of the normal personality range. In contrast to the medical approach which considers exception as an abnormality, this approach allows for the therapeutic view that strengthens self-esteem and self-confidence by providing experiences of success instead of attempting to reduce the symptoms of ADHD. As an example, in the Israeli army, soldiers and officers with ADHD are enabled to excel in demanding combat roles. Moreover, outstanding professional athletes like the basketball legend Michael Jordan have ADHD. Leading actors who have been diagnosed with ADHD have successfully channeled their abundant energy into highly acclaimed roles on the stage. These evidences show that therapeutic interventions for ADHD focusing on individual strengths and encouraging participation in activities where ADHD is an advantage, lead to experiences of personal success which in turn produce healthier, more constructive personal development.

Chapter 5

The subjective experience of people diagnosed with ADHD

In the previous chapters, a review was made for the diagnostic process, a distinction was made between inattention and lack of concentration due not to Attention Deficit Hyperactivity Disorder (ADHD) but to other disorders, and accepted treatment interventions were overviewed. The review was done from the perspective of researchers using quantitative research and professionals working in the field.

In the current chapter, however, the perspective of those who diagnosed with ADHD is presented, examining how they view the disorder and its treatment. This is presented through stories of their subjective experience of the diagnostic process, the meaning they attribute to the diagnosis, how they cope with their difficulties, their experiences regarding drug therapy, how ADHD affects learning, and their overall quality of life.

It is important to note that, relative to the vast amount of research in the field, t few studies directly examine the self-experience of people with ADHD. One reason is likely because diagnosis and treatment predominantly occurs in childhood, with a focus on learning difficulties. When the dominant perception is that children's experiences are inaccurate, research neglects a complete examination of the aspects of ADHD and its outcomes and what is good for the children, especially in the long term. Accordingly, most research has focused on the objective aspects of the disorder and its implications for the future than on the perception of children, examined with through qualitative research. This aims to help the professionals and parents responsible for children's education and outcomes.

However, self-experience-focused research is an important addition to objective research, because the children subjective perspective can produce much information and lead to a better understanding of diagnosis and its implications. In addition, the contribution of drug treatment to functioning and self-experience in addressing challenges in many areas of life can be better understood.

Accordingly, the article below, published in a Hebrew psychology website in Israel (Avisar, 2014), applies a qualitative approach. This article in turn contains summaries of an article published in a scientific American journal (Avisar & Lavie, 2014). In this article, 14 adolescents diagnosed with ADHD in childhood were interviewed about their own experiences. Permission from the website and the journal to use these data was given.

The experience of adolescents diagnosed with ADHD

By Dr. Alon Avisar

Abstract

This study describes the experiences of adolescents with ADHD regarding the diagnostic process and drug treatment. Fourteen interviews were conducted with adolescents diagnosed with ADHD, and the data were analyzed using a phenomenological qualitative approach. The results showed that the adolescents were passive in the diagnostic process, with a limited attitude regarding their diagnosis. Regarding their drug treatment experience (all were treated by stimulant medications), half reported that the treatment helped them with studies and tests, but most commented on side effects including fatigue, identity change, and lack of desire for social participation. In the transition to junior high school, the adolescents significantly reduced the drug treatment, especially voluntarily, with some of the adolescents continuing to selectively take the stimulant medications during tests.

Introduction

Attention Deficit Hyperactivity Disorder (ADHD) is one of the most common disorders among children and adolescents, with its prevalence ranging from 3–20% (Polanczyk, Silva de Lima, Bernardo, Biederman, & Rohde, 2010). The disorder is characterized by symptoms of inattention, lack of concentration, and hyperactive and impulsive behavior. Symptoms first appear in childhood and often persist into adolescence and adulthood (American Psychiatric Association, 2013).

Many studies have shown that children with ADHD experience difficulties concentrating and getting organized for learning and difficulty sitting for a long time, which often result in underachievement. In addition, hyperactive and impulsive symptoms often cause behavioral problems, conflicts with authority figures, and related social and emotional difficulties (Martel, Nigg, & Lucas, 2008; Semrud-Clikeman, Walkowiak, Wilkinson, & Minne, 2010).

Many studies have shown that drug treatment with stimulants such as Ritalin and similar medications is effective in reducing the symptoms of attention and concentration difficulties as well as of hyperactivity and impulsivity. In addition, the treatment results in marked improvement in learning and behavioral, social, and emotional functioning (Evans& Pelham, 2001; Powers, Marks, Miller, Newcorn, & Halperin, 2008; Swanson, Baler, & Volkow, 2011; Swanson et al., 2004). Over the past twenty years, there has thus been a sharp (250%) increase in the use of drug treatment in ADHD (Holden, Jenkins-Jones, Poole, Morgan, Coghill, & Currie, 2013).

However, most of the findings regarding drug efficacy have relied primarily on reports from parents, teachers, or professionals, while only a few studies have relied on reports from children and adolescents who used the treatment. Studies that consider also children's reports have found that children report less "benefit" and greater "cost" to medication than the reports of their parents.

For example, the main benefit reported by parents was an improvement in educational functioning, whereas children were more likely to report about the cost – side effects that include feelings of disconnection and personality change (Efron, Jarman & Barker, 1998; Harpur, Thompson, Daley, Abikoff & Sonuga-Barke, 2008; McNeal, Roberts & Barone, 2000). Moreover, children reported less improvement in quality of life as a result of stimulant medications and sometimes reported worse, especially in the social domain (for a review see, Coghill, 2010).

The purpose of this study is to further investigate how adolescents diagnosed with ADHD describe and experience the process of diagnosis and drug treatment. The research employed a qualitative approach in the form of interviews.

Method
Participants

IPA is an idiographic mode of inquiry, with studies conducted on small homogeneous samples to enable a detailed examination of how participants make sense of their lifeworld. Our study includes 14 adolescents who had been previously diagnosed with ADHD and used stimulant medications (some are no longer using medications). The interviewees were recruited through a private psychology center (when they arrived for a psych-didactic test), and some were recruited through acquaintances. The interviewees were eight boys and six girls who live in cities in central Israel, range in age from 12.5 to 16.5 years old, and are enrolled in mainstream education .Based on psychological diagnosis, all interviewees had an intelligence score within the normal range, and some of the interviewees had learning disorders in addition to ADHD. Participants were included if they (a) were in the seventh to eleventh grade; (b) were diagnosed with ADHD prior to high school; (c) were treated regularly for a period of at least six months; and (d) had no serious medical condition, comorbid psychopathology other than ADHD, or severe mood disorder. All the adolescents were diagnosed with ADHD by qualified neurologists and were recommended to be medicated with stimulant medications, that is, forms of methylphenidate (Ritalin, Ritalin-LA, Ritalin-SR, Concerta). Ten of the interviewees began regular medication after diagnosis in elementary school, and four were diagnosed and started taking medication in junior high school .This study was approved by a university ethical committee. The adolescents and their parents were informed about this study. After receiving the agreement of both the adolescents and their parents, the parents signed an informed consent form to participate in the research.

Data Collection and Analysis

The most common data collection method for IPA is semi-structured interviews. Semi-structured interviews allow the researcher and participant to engage in a flexible dialogue that encourages interviewees to offer their own ways of thinking and enable a deeper understanding between researcher and participant. A general interview schedule was employed consisting of open-ended questions. The interview was divided into three main sections to reflect the different aspects of treatment trajectories: the diagnosis, experiences of taking medication, and the withdrawal process or the continued use of the medication. Fourteen semi-structured interviews were conducted with the adolescents in the author's (AA's) clinic or at the interviewees' homes. The interviews lasted on average 45 minutes. Each interview was audiotaped and subsequently fully transcribed. The process of analysis followed Smith, Flowers, and Larkin's (2009) guidelines for IPA, beginning with a repeated reading of the transcript of each interview as new. Only after the analysis of each interview did we produce a consolidated table of themes and sub-themes for the group of participants as a whole. This table also contained a full matrix representing each interviewee's contribution. The themes were then combined, based on their prevalence and links, to form the subtheme and the main themes.

Findings

Three main themes emerged from the interviews: the process of the diagnosis and the implications of being diagnosed with ADHD, the experience of drug treatment, and the cessation of the drug treatment.

The process of diagnosis and the implications of being diagnosed with ADHD

The adolescents who were diagnosed as young children hardly remembered what they were told about the meaning of the disorder. Even those diagnosed at a later age did not know much about the diagnostic process, and some said they did not receive much of an explanation about the disorder. Most of the adolescents said that their parents explained that they were taking them for testing so they could concentrate better. One of the girls said, "I was not told exactly what it was, they told me I had attention problems. Hmm . . . not so much explained . . . explained to my mother. They told me there was a pill which will help me concentrate. I went to the clinic, they checked me and said I needed to take a medication. I took until sixth grade and then I quit." A teenager diagnosed in junior high school said, "I was seated on a computer and I had to click when a certain figure appeared. I was then told that I have ADHD. I was told I would take a low dose medication, both because of my weight and because I had a marginal results in the test."

The statements were limited in contents. The adolescents seem to have very passively experienced the diagnostic process and reported mostly remembering what they were told about the end result and the treatment. From their statements, it does not appear that they received an explanation about what ADHD is and what it means to be diagnosed with it.

Regarding the feeling about their diagnosis, few adolescents (boys or girls) reported being ashamed of their diagnosis and their drug treatment. Some said that they felt different from everyone else at the time of the diagnosis, but most said that after realizing that many children are diagnosed with ADHD and receive drug treatment, they cared less about it: "A sorrow shared is a sorrow halved."

Here are some typical statements about the feeling regarding their diagnosis and their drug treatment:

"I was not ashamed at all. Everyone has attention difficulties, all of us. It's not something that embarrassed me, only in the beginning, in third grade, because I didn't understand what it was. I took 10 mg, which is the lowest. Not that I had a serious problem being hyperactive, I just don't like being quiet."

"At first I was a little ashamed of it ... but today I have no problem with it at all ... because today I realize I have no reason to be ashamed of it. Half of my friends takes Ritalin."

"I know a lot of friends who are diagnosed with ADHD, we don't talk about it and it's just not interesting. I am not ashamed because many from school are diagnosed with ADHD, it is common in many."

Regarding the effects of the disorder on their lives, most of the adolescents said that the disorder manifests primarily in difficulty concentrating and listening to the teacher at school, and less in daily life. For example, one of the adolescents said:

"I'm not focused in the classroom. Interrupting and talking with my friends. The teacher reads a story, and I feel it difficult to follow the story."

By contrast, one girl noted the behavioral consequences of the disorder:

"It was hard for me to sit for an hour on the chair and I wasn't concentrated at all." She continued, "They would also comment a lot on my behavioral problems ... being impudent and having outbursts. I burst out before someone [was] even done talking to me."

The adolescent's statements were often laconic, citing mainly the behavioral symptoms – inattention, impulsivity, and hyperactivity – as the main difficulties but not expanding much on the consequences of ADHD in their daily lives. In addition (despite being asked), the adolescents did not note frustrations or report seeing themselves as different because of the disorder. For example, one of girl noted:

"I think if I could say something to professionals who diagnose people with ADHD, then it's not to treat the children as if they're weird or have a problem, or like we're different. We're just the same with a little more energy [laughs]."

The drug treatment experience

Compared to their reports on the diagnostic process, adolescents provided more details on the drug treatment experience. Moreover, this issue seemed to concern them more than the diagnosis process.

Before presenting the results for each sub-topic – the effect of drug treatment on learning, the effect of drug treatment on the emotional state, and the effect of drug treatment on identity and on interpersonal relationships – it is important to note that all the adolescents used stimulant medications as their drug treatment. Most initially used the standard Ritalin, and two advanced to Ritalin-SR, three to Ritalin-LA, and three to Concerta upon reaching junior high school. (All these medications contain Methylphenidate as the active substance; this is similar to the standard Ritalin but has a longer duration. Ritalin-LA and Concerta are considered "gentler," with fewer side effects, than the standard Ritalin.)

It is also important to note that in junior high schools and high schools, there was a marked decrease in the consumption of the drug: Six adolescents completely stopped taking the medication, three continued to take the drug selectively – when they had to prepare for tests or during the tests themselves – and five adolescents continued to use the drug regularly (these were the youngest of the adolescents group).

1. The impact of drug therapy on learning – About half the adolescents said that drug therapy helped them to concentrate and learn better, while others said that it did not help them because they felt lethargic and tired. The following quotes are from the adolescents who claimed that the treatment helped them:

"The pills helped me to concentrate. At first I had headaches and nausea, but I take them for a long of time. So, I got used to it and now I feel nothing and it helps me at school."

"It's hard for me to concentrate. If one day I forgot to take the pill, in the classroom I try to concentrate and I feel that all the letters are floating in my head. It's hard to explain but it's impossible to concentrate, I mix the letters. When I take the pill, it helps me to concentrate significantly. I feel more in focus and I can do assignments."

The following are quotes from the adolescents who claimed that the drug treatment did not help them:

"It didn't help me in concentrating on the tests. I was told to take so I took. I haven't [taken] Ritalin for four years now because I think it doesn't help, it didn't do anything to me, just made me tired. "In school, it would make me tired and I would feel uncomfortable, I used to put my head down on the table and go to sleep. I saw that it didn't help me learn better."

"In classes I wasn't taking out notebooks because I was not strong enough to take out the notebook. I was in a completely different world, I had headaches so I could not listen, pay attention, take out notebooks. With the pill, in the morning I used to eat the biggest meal I can, not the biggest, a big meal, and then I used to take the pill and goes to school [and sit] on the chair and put my head on my hands, until the break. I didn't do anything and didn't move. I didn't move a millimeter and then when the break comes. I used to go up the stairs, and sit on them until the break ends."

2. The effect of drug treatment on emotional state – All of the adolescents reported that they used to experience side effects that included abdominal pain, loss of appetite, and sometimes dizziness of varying intensity. Some of the adolescents became accustomed to the side effects and reported normal functioning under the influence of the drug treatment. However, most of the adolescents reported experiences that affected their emotional state, such as sleepiness and low motivation. Some of the boys also described a depressive condition under the influence of the drug. It is important to note that most of the adolescents who reported positive effects in learning also reported the side effects and emotional states described above. In addition, there were no general differences in these experiences between adolescents who consumed the different kinds of methylphenidate stimulant medications were used in this study.

The following statements describe the emotional experience of the drug treatment that was common to several adolescents:

"In third grade, when I was taking the pill, I was feeling drowsy and lost my appetite. I felt like I was in a dream. I told my parents and they said it's a pill that helps, you just have to get used to it I sat quietly, feeling like I am on some kind of anesthesia. Parents don't know what it is, if they had taken it once they would have known. I always said to my mom, 'Try to take, feel what I feel.' Feeling nasty, like there's something in you and you're in a bubble. Don't feel like do things or get out. What you're looking for is just lying down, and not doing anything. It helps parents; if you are at home, you will be quiet."

"You are depressed. There is no desire for anything and you do not want to do anything. You just want to rest, you have no appetite."

"Regularly when I take Ritalin, I have abdominal pain. It block[s] my appetite. Sometimes I have dizziness . . . sometimes it also affects my mood . . . I don't always have the desire for friends and sometimes I'm just feeling down for no reason."

"I go through a few classes and I can't eat because of that. I keep drinking but my headache's doesn't go. I come home tired too, and at school it gives you a feeling that it helps but it doesn't really help."

"From the first grade, every day I used to take Ritalin, I don't think it helped me. I just used to sit in the classroom, even more tired, thinking about nothing, I didn't eat, I played football like a drunk with Ritalin. Felt Less hunger and more fatigue with no desire to do anything."

"I didn't feel like eating. I felt dizzy and headache, like I'm going to pass out if I will make quick movements. Also strong pains, dizziness too. When I got up from the chair everything spins."

3. The effect of drug treatment on identity and interpersonal relationships – Most of the adolescents who had continuous side effects discussed characteristics related to their sense of identity and their functioning in interpersonal situations. In terms of identity, they sometimes said that they had experienced a sense of disconnection and that their temperaments have changed from energetic to quiet, including a decline in their desire to communicate. Socially, the adolescents said that their desire to be around and hang out with people had decreased and they routinely sought more peace and quiet surroundings.

The following examples describe the adolescents' experiences with their sense of identity and their interpersonal relationships under the influence of the drug treatment:

"You feel like you are in your own world when you take Ritalin, like you are in a bubble. Talking to you and you really . . . that's not. It . . . it's a real difference, like you are outside of the curriculum. . . . It was shocking, it wasn't me. It's just felt like they took a shot and injected it to me . . . that's just how I felt. When I was taking, I was really quiet and not talking to people, and when I wasn't taking I had energy. But when you eat before and the Ritalin stops, then you become who you were before. It's important to eat before that."

"Without the medication I went to friends, we walked downstairs, laughed and all kinds. When I was with the medication, I didn't have the strength to go down, I didn't have the strength to go to study."

However, one girl talked about how the drug treatment helped her regulate aggressive behaviors in social interactions, leading her to see it as a positive thing:

"Without the Ritalin I act just as I once did before I was start taking Ritalin. But it's good because the dizziness, stomach aches and my appetite goes back. However, it's hard for me to control my reactions when I am without Ritalin. I am impudent and I burst out before someone finish talking to me . . . hey [laughing] it's good and bad together."

The adolescents who have been taking drug treatments for years appear to have had difficult experiences, and it seems that this has not been sufficiently considered. The issue here is not whether the drug treatment is good, but rather that children's experiences should be taken seriously. These difficult experiences, which in some cases cause great suffering, can lead even to issues of distrust.

The cessation of the drug treatment

As noted above, upon reaching junior high school, there was a marked decrease in the adolescents' drug treatment consumption. However, in the transition to high school, some have used the stimulant medications selectively to prepare for and take tests.

Here is an example of a girl who decided to stop taking the drug:

> *"I felt like I am on some kind of anesthetic. At first I took half a pill for three months and then I started to get a whole pill. There were times I dodged, I have said that I took and I didn't take until I was caught, or thrown it into the bin and finally told my mom the truth. Finally she gave up when I said, 'Let me succeed without it.' In fourth and sixth grade, I always escaped taking it but in seventh grade I got to the point that I didn't want it anymore. Socially it didn't help, it just made me get into myself and not talk. I'm not a quiet person, but today as an adult, I realizes that you have to sit quietly in class."*

From this comment and those of others, it appears that the transition to adolescence seems to change the positions of the participants on consumption of the drug. This manifests in taking an active stance regarding the drug treatment consumption and in their attitude toward coping with the demands of reality. Thus, if they feel that they do not derive a significant benefit from the drug treatment, they decide to stop using it. However, when they feel that they do get a significant benefit from the drug treatment, they voluntarily take it and see it as a key to success in their studies. The following is a typical example in this regard:

> *"When you [are] cramming and do final exams – yes to take it – but when you don't, then no. I do take it when I have cramming and going through final tests, but on normal days when I finish school at 12:45, I don't take it."*

Discussion

The purpose of this study was to examine what adolescents with ADHD relate about their experiences from the time of the diagnosis of the disorder and during the period when they received the drug treatment. The results show that the adolescents described the diagnostic process laconically. They also mentioned that they did not remember having the diagnosis explained to them. In addition, from their descriptions, it seems that they were passive in the diagnostic process, without much involvement and without a substantial attitude toward the issue. Their young age during the diagnostic process might have influenced their ability to remember and understand the process, although the adolescents who were diagnosed at a relatively late age also described the process in this laconic manner.

In addition, most of them were not ashamed of being diagnosed, because they realized that many children they knew were also have the diagnosis. As mentioned, ADHD is one of the most common disorders among children and adolescents, with a prevalence of 3–20% in the western developed countries (Polanczyk et al., 2010). In Israel, the prevalence of diagnosed and drug treated children is similar to the developed countries (Fogelman, Vinker, Guy & Kahan, 2003; Vinker, Vinker & Elhayany, 2006). It is thus unsurprising that the adolescents who participated in this study knew many children who were also diagnosed and felt that they were not exceptional.

In contrast to how they described the diagnostic process, most discussed their drug treatment enthusiastically, and it appeared that some were discussing it for the first time. For some, it was important to describe the negative effects of the stimulant medications, whose physical side effects include headaches, dizziness, and loss of appetite. The negative effects described included a sense of identity change, mood decline, and unwillingness to participate in social interactions.

Regarding the effect of the drug treatment on learning, about half the adolescents claimed that the drug treatment helped them to concentrate, remember, and learn better in the short term. Their feelings about the effect of the drug treatment on learning are consistent with the findings of many studies that have shown that stimulant medications are effective in reducing ADHD symptoms and improving concentration and function in learning (Evans & Pelham, 2001; Swanson et al., 2004; Swanson et al., 2011). However, other claimed that the drug treatment did not help them because the side effects caused them to perform poorly. Similarly to this findings, further studies have reported a decline in performance in some children who have treated with stimulant medications (Efron et al., 1998; Harpur et al., 2008; McNeal et al., 2000). Further discussion about this disparity, will take place later.

Regarding long-term educational and functional improvement, some of the adolescents reported that the drug treatment did not significantly improve their long-term achievement, this was true especially of those diagnosed with additional learning difficulties. These reports are also consistent with studies that found that regular and prolonged drug treatment does not improve long-term learning and functioning, especially when there are an additional learning disorders and difficulties (Gittelman, Klein, & Feingold, 1983; Powers et al., 2008).

Regarding the drug treatment experiences, some of the adolescents mentioned common and transient side effects, such as abdominal pain and loss of appetite. Several, however, also reported experiencing despondency, powerlessness, and reluctance to participate in activities they love such as sports activities. In addition, they related feelings of disconnection and change in identity and personality. These changes were characterized by passivity, unwillingness to talk much, and a decreased desire to participate in social events. They mentioned that these negative effects did not characterize them prior to taking the drug treatment or without its influence. They described these feelings as unpleasant, and some said that they just waited for the effects of the drug to pass to return to their normal state.

Similarly to the findings of the present study, further studies have reported feelings of disconnection, personality change, and lack of motivation to participate in activities among children who have treated with stimulant medications (Efron et al., 1998; Harpur et al., 2008; McNeal et al., 2000). For example, in one study, interviews were conducted with adult students with ADHD who were asked about their experience with drug treatment from childhood through being students. Most of them discussed unpleasant experiences in childhood under the influence of stimulant medications: a feeling of disconnection and apathy, a sense of identity change, a general slowness, and a decreased desire to work. Moreover, some students said that the drugs made it difficult for them to engage in social interaction, since they felt disconnected, as if they were in a bubble, thus reducing their social ability to communicate (Meaux, Hester, Smith, & Shoptaw, 2006).

In contrast to the findings of the present study, many studies describe a significant reduction in ADHD symptoms, better learning, increased emotional and behavioral functioning, and experiences of success and self-esteem as a result of drug treatment in ADHD (Evans & Pelham, 2001; Swanson et al., 2004; Swanson et al., 2011). The question arises as to why there is such a difference between the results of, on the one hand, studies that found improvement in learning and functioning and experiences of success and, on the other hand, studies that found side effects of impaired functioning, as in the present study. One factor that may explain this inconsistency is that, generally, the studies that showed significant improvements have only children who took regular drug treatment and for whom the treatment was found to be effective (Coghill, 2010; ; Powers et al., 2008; Swanson et al., 2001). These studies thus did not include children whose drug treatment did not significantly improve their function and who therefore stopped using it. This exclusion criteria contrasted with the current study, which included and described the experiences of adolescents who felt that the treatment did not aid them and therefore stopped using it or began to use it selectively. Moreover, in studies that showed significant improvement, the improvement was reported by teachers and parents and not by the children themselves. In the few studies that have examined the reports of both children and parents, children were indeed found to report less improvement in quality of life and social situations and to focus more on side effects compared to their parents, who focused more on learning improvements (Coghill, 2010; Efron et al., 1998; Harpur et al., 2008; McNeal et al., 2000).

Another finding of the present study was a marked decrease in the use of stimulant medications in the transition from elementary school to junior high school, or the transition from junior high school to high school among the adolescents who were diagnosed at the beginning of the junior high school. Some explained that they were already reluctant to take the stimulant medications in elementary school because of the unwanted side effects but that because of their young age they had no choice, as it was not up to them but to their parents. Later, when they became adolescents and progressed to junior high school, they were able to persuade their parents to reduce the drug treatment. This finding is consistent with those of other studies: As parental dependence decreases, there is a decline in drug treatment use (Harpuret al., 2008; Hazell, 2007; Meaux et al., 2006).

In addition, in high school, some of the adolescents continued to take the medications selectively, when they needed to prepare for and perform better on tests. They reported voluntarily taking the stimulant medications when they needed to prepare for final exams, since the stimulant medications helped them concentrate. It seems that when it is important for the adolescents to succeed in learning, they see more of the benefits of stimulant medications in terms of improvement and focus less on the costs in the form of side effects.

Conclusions and recommendations

The above indicates that children and adolescents diagnosed with ADHD do not know enough about their disorder and its consequences. Therefore, more explanation for the adolescents is needed throughout the diagnostic process. This is important to help children better know themselves and their strengths and weaknesses.

In addition, it appear that some children have been taking drug treatments for years and have had difficult experiences. The issue here is not whether the drug treatment is good but rather that children's experiences should be taken seriously. Therefore, monitoring the cost and benefit of drug treatment in the educational, emotional, behavioral, and social areas should be seriously considered.

CHAPTER 6

ADHD as a social and cultural phenomenon

From the previous chapters it can be seen that the validity of ADHD as a disorder with a solid and specific etiology is disputable both in terms of observed behavioral symptoms and their relation to cognitive functions which are measurable by neuropsychological tasks, brain imaging, hereditary factors and drug treatments.

1. It has been found that the behavioral symptoms of inattention, impulsivity and hyperactivity associated with ADHD are not exclusive to it and are found with high frequency in numerous situations, difficulties and disorders. Even a simple headache or fatigue may produce restlessness, difficulty in concentration, irritability and a tendency toward impulsiveness just as deep, emotionally-driven psychiatric disorders like depression, anxiety, and emotional overload do. The general feeling of negativity and frustration in dealing with learning disorders, sleeping disorders and other

behavioral disorders also gives rise to these symptoms. As all the above, especially in children can present with a clinical picture of restlessness and difficulty in concentration, a misdiagnosis of ADHD is a frequent risk (DSM-V; American Psychiatric Association, 2013).

2. Numerous studies have been conducted to find a relation between specific cognitive deficits using neuropsychological tests and the behavioral symptoms of ADHD. It has been determined (in contrary to intuition) that the ability for selective attention, that is, the ability to find a specific target amid distractors is not the major disability underlying ADHD. Hence, research has focused more on impairment in executive functioning that can be measured by cognitive testing. Executive functions includes response inhibition, regulation of emotions and behavior, working memory, mental flexibility, and the ability to plan. Although people with ADHD do indeed show impairment in various executive functions, not everyone diagnosed with ADHD suffers from impaired executive functioning. Moreover, people with ADHD exhibit disability in different executive functions. Deficits in executive functioning have also been found in in children with dyslexia, autism, Obsessive-Compulsive Disorder (OCD), and depression. Among people with ADHD the deficits in executive functioning show great heterogeneity. It is known that intelligence and learning disorders also affect this relation (Seidman, 2006). The research proves that there is no difference in executive functioning between the two different presentations or subtypes of ADHD (inattention vs. hyperactivity and impulsivity). Thus, even if a relation between deficits in executive functioning and ADHD does exist, it is not specific, nor is it exclusive or sufficient enough. For this reason, ADHD cannot be diagnosed solely on tests

which measure executive functioning. Once again, there is no certainty that disability in executive functioning is a definitive indicator of ADHD. There is widespread scientific accord that even if cognitive deficits have been detected by neuropsychological testing, they, in and of themselves, do not provide sufficient evidence for an ADHD diagnosis.

3. Numerous studies involving brain imaging have been conducted in the attempt to understand the relation between ADHD and brain structure and function. It was found that people with ADHD have lower brain activity in certain areas of the brain: the frontal and prefrontal lobes of the brain, the limbic system, the basal ganglia and the cerebellum. These are the regions of the brain responsible, among other things, for arousal and attention, executive functioning, regulation of behavior and emotions and response inhibition. Although impairment in brain activity was found to be pronounced in children with severe ADHD and low intelligence (IQ), the findings on brain activity in adults with ADHD were inconsistent. In addition, studies using brain imaging have not yet found a difference between the different presentations of ADHD: ADHD with inattention and hyperactivity and impulsivity and ADHD with inattention but without hyperactivity and impulsivity presentations. Moreover, impaired activity in the areas of the brain associated with ADHD have also been observed in other disorders such as: communication disorders such as autism, Obsessive-Compulsive Disorder (OCD), bipolar disorder (manic-depression) and other disorders. For this reason, attempts to detect and diagnose ADHD exclusively through brain scans have been unsuccessful. Thus, despite its contribution to the etiology of ADHD by detecting structures and functions with impaired brain

activity, the results obtained from brain imaging are too heterogeneous to be considered definitive. To date brain imaging has not been able to detect exclusive areas of brain malfunction that are distinct to ADHD relative to other disorders. Similarly, studies have failed to show differences in brain activity between the two different presentations of ADHD. Hence, an etiology specific to ADHD alone has not been detected.

4. Genetic studies have shown that ADHD is one of the most hereditary disorders which "run in the family". Although several genes may be involved, research cannot point to a specific gene and the several genes that seem to be related to ADHD are only weakly so. Moreover, this group of genes was found to be equally related to other disorders as well. The difficulty in finding a specific ADHD-related gene is a product of the diversity and variability of the behavioral symptoms of ADHD and its co-morbidities. Similarly, environmental factors that seem to be related to ADHD are not unique to it and were influencers in many other disorders. These factors seem to correlate more with the co-morbidities of ADHD. Hence, they do not sufficiently explain the etiology of ADHD.

Thus, despite the vast research regarding the causes of ADHD, a factor that is exclusive and specific has not yet been found. Hence, the view of ADHD as a distinct disorder engendered by well-determined circumstances is controversial (Lindstrøm, 2012). As no region of the brain or cognitive difference was found in the different presentations of ADHD, that is, no differences were found in the causes or mediators of the different presentations (subtypes) of ADHD: ADHD with attention deficit and with hyperactivity and impulsivity presentations or presentation of ADHD with inattention but without hyperactivity and impulsivity, the distinction between these presentations may be a mere convenience for behavioral and symptomatic diagnoses and their association with various co-morbidities. The stability and etiologic validity of these presentations seems unjustified (Willcuet et al., 2012).

Common myths about ADHD

Despite extensive research and information on ADHD, myths about the disorder persist, that create false representation and misinformation about ADHD. Perhaps lack of prominence of relevant research or equivocal findings that leave room for other explanations are responsible. In any case, these myths can mislead and cause a misunderstanding of ADHD and its treatments, so it is necessary to debunk these myths.

Here are some common myths:
1. One of the main myths is that the "("attention deficit "). AD" in the acronym implies that the deficit underlying the behavioral symptoms of the disorder is cognitive inattention, or the inability to focus and ignore distracters (selective attention). Explicitly, this refers to difficulty in recognizing reality clearly and correctly when perceiving significant amounts of non-filtered stimuli. This leads to high distraction. A comparison has sometimes been made to a short-sighted person who urgently needs glasses in order to function properly (glasses being an analog to medication). Despite the intuitive logic behind this myth and the comparison, it is false. Already by the 1980s, researchers were aware that the cognitive tests that measure selective attention do not significantly differentiate between people with ADHD and people without it (Avisar, 2011; Van der Meere & Sergeant, 1988). Accordingly, Huang-Pollock et al. (2005) conclude that, in contrary to logic, tests of

selective attention do not prove that a deficit in selective mental attention is the core deficit underlying ADHD. The fact that children with ADHD have no problems in playing video games demonstrates the notion that selective cognitive attention is not the main deficit in ADHD. Further support is derived from the fact that a high percentage of elite athletes (including the legendary basketball player Michael Jordan) have been diagnosed with ADHD and they have no difficulty in identifying targets, ignoring distracters or responding quickly and accurately to relevant stimuli.

2. Another myth related to the various presentations of ADHD states that people with the inattentive presentation of ADHD have a deficit in selective or sustained attention while people with ADHD who present with hyperactivity and impulsivity have a deficit in response inhibition, which is considered an executive function. However, since no difference in cognitive functioning as measured by neuropsychological tests or brain imagery was found in people with the two different behavioral presentations, this myth is untrue. it has been argued that this distinction is just a convenience for making a symptomatic diagnosis and relating it to various co-morbidities. The etiological validity of these presentations is unjustified (Willcutt et al., 2012).

3. Another myth is that ADHD is a sub-category of learning disorders and has a specific and direct relation to reading, writing and arithmetic. This is probably due to the fact that learning disorder, one of the common co-morbidities of ADHD has an estimated 16-48% correlation to childhood ADHD (Wei et al., 2014). However, the theoretical mechanisms underlying learning disorders differ from those of ADHD. Reading and writing disorders are most often due to difficulties

in Phonological language mechanisms or the result of lexical difficulties. In contrast, ADHD, at least theoretically is a result of impairment in executive function with no causal relation to language or lexical mechanisms. Consequently, learning disorders and ADHD are classified under separate categories according to the DSM. The reason why so many children with ADHD are diagnosed with learning disorder is probably related to the burden that their difficulties in concentration place upon effective learning, resulting in under achievements. Or, alternatively, since children with learning disorder evince frustration and avoidance due to their learning difficulties, they may seem not to be able to concentrate and therefore, exhibit restlessness. These children are probably misdiagnosed with ADHD. The high variability in the studies relating ADHD to learning disorders reinforce this presumption. In addition, it is important to note once again that drug treatment does not significantly improve learning outcomes in children diagnosed with ADHD and learning disorders (Gittelman et al., 1983; Grizenko et al., 2006).

4. Another common myth is that stimulant medications are only effective for people with ADHD. This myth is not true because studies show that stimulant medications improve the concentration of both children and adults without ADHD as well. As mentioned in the Chapter 4, as early as World War II stimulants were used to improve the alertness of German civilians and soldiers who were controllers, lookouts and fighters. In addition, many students without ADHD use stimulants to achieve better outcomes on tests. Many adults without ADHD use these drugs to maintain concentration at work (Rasmussen, 2008). Stimulants are known to improve

athletic performance and to reduce recovery time in sports injuries. For this reason, they are on the list of prohibited substances in professional sport competitions. It is also important to emphasize that a positive response to stimulant medications is not an indication for a diagnosis of ADHD.

Prevalence of ADHD

Although there are still many unresolved questions about the etiology, diversity and inclusiveness of the behavioral symptoms of ADHD and the effectiveness of long-term drug treatment, ADHD is still the most prevalent childhood disorder. It ranges from 8-12% of the population and exhibits high variation among countries and cultures (Biederman & Faraone, 2005). In some regions the variation is 1.7-17.8% (Rowland et al., 2002). The estimated number of children diagnosed with ADHD in the US, according to a national 2016 parent survey is 9.4% (6.1 million) (Danielson et al., 2018). In Israel, the prevalence is 9.5% in the Jewish sector (almost 1 in 10, close to that of the US and other Western countries) and 7.35% in the Arab sector (Ornoy et al., 2016).

For children with ADHD drug treatment is the therapy most frequently applied. Stimulant medications have been prescribed for over 50 years and their use has increased by hundreds of percentage points in the last twenty years. Use of stimulant medications is highest in the United States. In Europe it is significantly lower (Beau-Lejdstrom, Douglas, Evans, & Smeeth, 2016). In two states in the United States, drug treatment for ADHD included 8-10% of the primary school population (LeFever, Dawson & Morrow, 1999). In 2016, 62% of children diagnosed with ADHD in the US were on ADHD medications (Danielson et al., 2018). A survey conducted in Israel by the Maccabi HMO which included 284,419 children, found that 12.6% of children diagnosed with ADHD, and 8.5% of children so diagnosed were prescribed ADHD medication, although in practice only 4.8% took their medication regularly (Cohen et al., 2013). Furthermore, a significantly higher proportion of relatively younger children being diagnosed with ADHD and/or receiving medication for this. The relative age effect is well demonstrated in countries with known higher prescribing rates (Holland & Sayal, 2019).

The development of the ADHD phenomenon

A question arises as to why the ADHD diagnosis and the preferred treatment via drug therapy have increased by hundreds of percentage points in the last twenty years and as to how ADHD has become the most prevalent childhood disorder in the Western world.

Here are a few explanations:
1. ADHD is characterized by a variety of behaviors and these can also be the result of many other disorders and difficulties. In addition, ADHD has two types of presentations and their symptomatic heterogeneity is co-terminus with several of its co-morbidities. This blurs the diagnostic boundary and even makes that boundary subjective. While it is difficult to diagnose whether a symptom is the specific result of ADHD, it is easy to diagnose a clinical expression of ADHD even without knowing whether it is a result of ADHD. "Wherever you throw a stone, you hit a target."

    For example. take the hypothetical case of a 9-year-old child in a third-grade class of 35 students. As at this age educational demands increase, social involvement becomes more meaningful and social conflict and annoyances typical of this age often prevail, a child with learning difficulties may get involved in typical third-grade personality clashes and may sometimes even behave aggressively. Emotionally, the child is frustrated by the situation and may be on edge. This child may not be too interested in learning and is certainly not persistent in completing homework independently. Parental mediation to promote homework completion creates additional friction at home. If this child is referred for a professional diagnosis, the following clinical expressions of ADHD that accord with the symptoms and criteria of the disorder in the DSM-V appear: Difficulty in persevering, difficulty in concentrating, difficulty in completing tasks, avoidance of assignments, avoidance of homework, distractedness, restlessness, and impulsivity. Moreover, as the symptoms exists for at least six months and in at least two different places, school and home, the teacher and parent questionnaires probably strengthen the assessment. The likelihood of this child receiving an ADHD diagnosis with or without hyperactivity is high.

Since the prevalence of ADHD at this age is approximately 10% and this is the age when receipt of a diagnosis of ADHD is at its height (LeFeveret al., 1999), there is a strong probability that two more children from this child's class will be diagnosed with ADHD as well. To determine whether this child really has ADHD, a comprehensive history must be taken along with administration of the cognitive and emotional examinations described in Chapter 1. Alternative explanations for the difficulties presented must be ruled out.

2. There is a wide experiential gap between conventional pedagogy and the excitement provided by the technological devices that entertain children today. These devices enable quicker, more intense stimulation than the deliberate, slower-paced transmission of information in schools. This disparity makes school

environments seem dull and can create low motivation for studying (Beyers, 2009). Hence, the challenge for today's children— sitting quietly for long periods of time, learning and listening to teachers in classrooms of 35 children— is greater than ever before. It produces an environment in which large numbers of children find it difficult to concentrate and those children who have the most difficulty can appear as being symptomatic of ADHD.

3. The relation between ADHD and behavioral problems: one of the common co-morbidities for the hyperactive and impulsivity presentation of ADHD is behavioral problems (Gaub & Carlson, 1997). Today's over-crowded classrooms place a limit on teachers' tolerance for misbehavior, especially since instituting programs that counter behavioral problems require a great deal of time, effort and commitment. They also require above-board cooperation between teachers and parents which is sometimes difficult to achieve. In addition, teachers often deal with several children with behavioral problems in the class, so the difficulty and the complexity of achieving a solution only increase. All the above make a diagnosis of ADHD with an accompanying prescription for medication a tempting recourse (Santosh & Taylor, 2000). It is important to note that the DSM-V distinguishes between behavioral problems that produced by ADHD and those that are not and emphasizes that behavioral problems which at first glance may seem as ADHD-related can cause a misdiagnosis if not thoroughly investigated. Because so many children with behavioral problems receive referrals for an ADHD assessment, the likelihood of misdiagnosis increase.

4. The demand for assessments often creates long queues at the HMO for specialists such as neurologists and

psychiatrists and may compel them to abbreviate their diagnostic processes. Statements from adolescents diagnosed with ADHD reveal that their diagnostic process consisted of only a short interview which was primarily concerned with difficulties in concentration (Avisar & Lavie, 2014). This narrow focus could, on its face lead to a misdiagnosis. Studies have corroborated that misdiagnoses of ADHD are associated with HMO overload and long queues (Kube, Petersen, & Palmer, 2002).

5. Stimulant medications "deliver the goods" in the short-term. They increase concentration, reduce hyperactivity and impulsivity, diminish behavioral problems and improve functioning in general. Unlike other medications, there is no need to wait a week or two until a positive effect is experienced. The effect occurs immediately upon ingestion. Nowadays the use of stimulant medication for study and work purposes, both with and without a prescription is widespread, even in people without ADHD. So whether or not a child has ADHD, the likelihood that by using stimulant medications, he or she will experience more concentration and will be able sit and study for longer periods of time is greater in the short-term. Thus, the temptation to use these "magical potions" in order to improve functioning increases.

The Causes of the ADHD phenomenon

The factors discussed above are the reasons for the readiness to diagnose and treat ADHD broadly. But over and above this, an ADHD diagnosis is incentivized by the following circumstances:

1. While the educational system is designed to deliver academic achievement, it is often difficult to cope with the overcrowding and the learning difficulties that

disturb both its sufferers and other students as well. Drug treatment brings about a quick and effective solution for reducing behavioral problems and improving children's educational functioning. Hence, the educational system has an incentive to recommend drug treatment as a quick solution for the demands placed upon it.

2. Understandably, parents have a desire to promote their children's success in the educational system. However, this sometimes conflicts with their children's learning difficulties. Thus, obtaining a medical diagnosis of ADHD may facilitate receiving an appropriate remedy to improve their children' function.

Since ADHD is seen by the public as a common – and perhaps even legitimate– disorder. As there is less stigma attached to the diagnosis and acceptance of the disorder is widespread, an ADHD diagnosis may even have positive appeal. Accordingly, it was found that adolescents with ADHD say that they are not ashamed of their diagnosis because many of their peers have received one as well (Avisar & Lavie-Ajayi, 2014). For parents, it is sometimes easier to accept a diagnosis of ADHD and its subsequent drug treatment because, in some cases, it supports their denial of other difficulties that are more complex and harder to treat. Since parents want their children to achieve, drug treatment can support their fantasy of having solved their child's difficulties by effecting significant improvement in a relatively uncomplicated way. For example, having a major learning disorder that manifests with considerable difficulty in reading is more challenging to deal with over time than a diagnosis of ADHD with its attendant drug treatment that brings hope that the reading difficulties will be resolved quickly. Obviously, if a learning disorder is the primary cause of a child's behavior problems, an ADHD diagnosis and subsequent drug treatment will have little effect in the log run.

3. Considering pharmaceutical companies' interest in high profits as any company, they want drug sales to be as sizeable as possible. Schwartz (The *New York Times*, 2013 and *The Marker*, 2013 in Hebrew in Israel) reported that in the US in 2012 sales of stimulants reached over $9 billion, a 500% jump over the preceding decade. Aggressive marketing by pharmaceutical companies include ad placements on TV, in women's magazines directed at mothers' concern for their children's success, and even in children's comic books and magazines. Consequently, the US Food and Drug Administration sued several big pharmaceuticals for false marketing practices that exaggerate these drugs' efficacy and play down their pernicious side effects. In addition, drug companies encourage physicians to attend conferences at luxury hotels in order to promote their drugs (Schwartz, 2013). Physicians acknowledge having received kickbacks for presenting drug treatments in a positive light to patients (Watson, Arcona, & Antonuccio, 2015).

4. As all scientists need to publish in order to advance their academic careers and require funding for their research, the pharmaceutical industry, with an obvious stake in the outcome of research into ADHD is a convenient resource for financing. Research is supposed to be bias-free and the source of its funding must be appended to each article. An examination of these appendices by Alon Avisar (the author of this book) reveals that almost all the research on drug treatment for ADHD was underwritten by a

pharmaceutical company. Here are a few examples from articles appendix about their research financial support: "Dr. _______ received a grant from Eli Lilly," "Ms. ____has received support for her salary from a NIMH grant from Eli Lilly," "________has received research support from Eli Lilly and Pfizer" (Eli Lilly and Pfizer are pharmaceutical companies). This does not mean that the studies were not done scrupulously, but it does illustrate the close linkage between the research industry and pharmaceutical companies, an association which may unconsciously weaken the objectivity of the research.

5. Professionals and private institutes for diagnosis and treatment in the private sector: the frequency of referrals for an ADHD diagnosis increases the scope of the private sector. Parents seeking results spend a lot of money on privately-funded assessments. These conducted by psychologists, psychiatrists, neurologists and consultants, who also perform computerized attention testing. This is in addition to the variously-priced drug treatments, alternative treatments, behavioral treatments, psychological treatments and others (Aharoni, 2013).

In light of the above, it would seem that the high prevalence of ADHD has generated high incentives and considerable financial return for those who deal in diagnosis and treatment for ADHD. Whether conscious or unconscious, the monetary interests are part of the social, cultural and commercial framework in which we live. While it's only natural that phenomena that generate profits and benefits for many parties would flourish. Since this, first and foremost is a phenomenon that a matter of children's health and development, caution should be exercised.

The following aspects of the treatment for ADHD should be examined:

- Are quality-of-life and children's educational and mental development being prioritized in all cases?
- Does overdiagnosis and overtreatment of ADHD contribute to education values?
- How does a misdiagnosis affect a child's development?
- How does a daily drug regimen which does not produce significant behavioral and academic improvement impact the educational and psychological development of the child?

These questions developed primarily from many studies that have raised suspicion about the accuracy of ADHD diagnoses (Beau-Lejdstromet al., 2016; Kubeet et al., 2002; LeFeveret et al., 1999; Schwartz, 2013). The above questions are generated by those studies that reveal that the greatest affirmative response to drug treatment occurs in people whose ADHD diagnosis is characterized by high hyperactivity, severe inattention and the absence of emotional disorders (Taylor & Taylor, 1999). But on the other hand, drug treatment is less effective for children with ADHD and learning disorders in conformance with the general profile of children with both ADHD and learning disorders who respond less well to stimulant medications and does not significantly show learning improvements than do children with ADHD but without learning disorders (Gittelman et al.,, 1983; Grizenko et al., 2006). In addition, the scientific consensus on improvement in learning after long-term drug treatment is not unanimous (Santosh & Taylor, 2000) especially since children with ADHD who were treated with stimulant medications over an extensive period continued to exhibit similar learning difficulty both at the end of primary school (van der Schanset al., 2017) and into high school (Powers et al., 2008).

Moreover, research about information from people with ADHD regarding their stimulant medication treatment reveals that such drug treatments have considerable negative side-effects. Besides the side effects such as headaches, nausea, dizziness, and sleep difficulty that usually disappear over time, more recusant effects of feelings of disconnection, personality changes and lack of motivation to participate in social activity persist (Efron et al., 1998; Harpur et al., 2008; McNeal et al., 2000). The improvement in children's quality-of-life as a result of using stimulant medications is ambiguous with some children reporting a worsening in social interactions (Coghill, 2010). Moreover, adult students with ADHD speak of unwanted childhood experiences under the influence of stimulant medications such as feelings of disconnection and apathy, a sense of their identity changing, general slowness and a lack of desire to work, difficulty in developing social connections because of feelings of disconnect— as if they "were in a bubble" (Meaux et al., 2006). Adolescents with ADHD report side-effects which include abdominal pain and loss of appetite, fatigue, a change in identity, depression of mood, and a lack of desire to participate in social activity. Educationally, about half of the adolescents claim that long-term drug treatment did not help them to achieve higher grades and that the side-effects of headache and fatigue caused a decline in function. Almost all the adolescents reported that while stimulant medications increased their short-term concentration, the persistent side effects coupled with their decreased motivation to participate in social activities led to a reduced desire to take the medication (Avisar & Lavie-Ajayi, 2014).

In addition, there is abundant evidence that many children seek to discontinue their medication. Accordingly, adolescents said that they wanted to stop the drug treatment in their childhood but had difficulty in persuading their parents to allow them to do so. However, in the transition to the junior high school, most of these adolescents significantly reduced their drug intake by their own volition as they succeeded in convincing their parents to allow them to do so at last (Avisar & Lavie-Ajayi, 2014; for an Abstract in Hebrew see, Avishar, 2014). In accordance, further studies have shown that there is a significant decline in the use of drug treatments in the transition from adolescence to adulthood, a period when parental authority decreases (Harpuret al., 2008; Meauxet al., 2006; Price et al., 2020). In addition, it is important to note that, only a small proportion of adolescents who stopped ADHD medication subsequently resumed their prescriptions in primary care (Newlove-Delgado et al., 2019).It is important to note the inherent contradiction between studies that report negative experiences with stimulants among people with ADHD and many other studies that indicate marked improvement in functioning of people with ADHD, following drug treatment. This discrepancy may be due to the fact that the studies that report improvement were based on interviews with parents and teachers whose major concern seemed to be improvement in learning outcomes while those studies that focused on the self-reports of children with ADHD were more critical of the social costs and the pernicious side-effects of stimulants. In addition, many of the studies emphasizing the marked improvement in academic functioning primarily focused on those children whose drug treatment was effective and who consumed the drugs regularly for a specified period of time (Coghill, 2010). However, they did not include children with ADHD whose drug treatment did not produce significant improvement and who as a consequence did not take their medication regularly. Moreover, the studies with positive results were generally measured the short-term specific effects, relative to studies that describe experiences where in drug treatment did not contribute to either improved long-term functioning or improved quality-of-life in general. The discrepancy stems from the different effects of the drug treatments. While drug treatment significantly increased concentration and functioning in the short-term, which is very impressive and even "magical," various negative long-term effects sometimes so impaired functioning that there were difficulties in adhering to a regular regimen. Hence, like everything else, drug treatment for ADHD has costs and benefits. Both should be considered when deciding whether to take it.

Conclusion

As we can see, the outlook on ADHD diagnoses and the efficacy of drug treatment is complex. The diagnosis is complex since the symptoms of ADHD are common to many other disorders besides ADHD. Thus, without conducting an in-depth examination, it is easy to misdiagnose ADHD. We also can see that even though drug treatment significantly increases functioning in the short-term, long-term improvement is often negligible. furthermore, medications are much less effective if the dysfunction is due to a learning disorder or learning difficulty or major emotional difficulty. Or sometimes due to the negative effects of medication present a cost in domains other than learning, namely in children's quality-of-life.

And yet, despite these Abundant findings, there is insufficient regulation of ADHD diagnoses and treatments. Like any other disorder, ADHD is supposed to have a maximum frequency no greater than 5%. Yet, the rate of diagnosis is much higher than that. According to the scientific approach, a deviation larger than 5% from the average of the general population is insignificant. That is, if a disorder has a prevalence greater than 5%, it, by definition becomes a phenomenon.

Since, some people with ADHD exhibit frustration, disappointment, and distrust as a result of taking daily doses of medication over several years without making significant advances in their studies and while encountering many pernicious side-effects along the way. They quit the drug treatment only when they got older and are in a position to decide for themselves whether to continue (Avisar & Lavie-Ajayi, 2014). Hence, it is very important to scrutinize the course of drug treatments to ensure that they contribute to healthy personal development.

Therefore, my recommendations for parents, educators, and professionals are: Be advised that not every child who has difficulty concentrating in school has ADHD. Accordingly, it is important to get to the root of the inability to maintain attention and not to decide *a priori* that a child has ADHD. Concerted effort must be put forth to obtain a correct diagnosis and to finding an appropriate therapeutic intervention.

Regarding the drug treatment, since the financial and psychological cost of a maintaining a regimen of daily medication which may include pernicious side-effects may be high, continuous monitoring that takes into consideration the child's self-reports is required. Continuation or cessation of drug treatments should depend on the minimization of pernicious side-effects along with the benefits achieved in educational, emotional, social and behavioral domains. It is important to focus on the child's strengths and interests, rather than employing a deficit-focused medical approach. Promoting the child's own desires encourages the child's intrinsic motivation. This leads to experiences of personal success which in turn produce healthier, more constructive personal development.

References

Achenbach, T. M., & Recorla, L. A. (2001). *Manual for the ASEBA School-Age Forms & Profiles.* Burlington University of Vermont, Reaserch Center for Children, Youth, & Families.

Aharoni A. (2013). *Does the child have attention deficit disorder? Get ready to pay hundreds and thousands of shekels.* Retrieved from https://www.globes.co.il/news/article.aspx?did=1000 888869

Ahikam, M. D. (2013). *People with ADHD will be able to serve in combat units.* Retrieved from https://www.makorrishon.co.il/nrg/online/1/ART2/ 428/505.html

Akutagava-Martins, G. C., Salatino-Oliveira, A., Kieling, C. C., Rohde, L. A., &Hutz, M. H. (2013). Genetics of attention-deficit/hyperactivity disorder: current findings and future directions. *Expert Review of Neurotherapeutics, 13*(4), 435-45.

American Psychiatric Association. (2000). *Diagnostic and statistical manual of mental disorders (4th ed., Text Rev.).* Washington, DC: Author.

American Psychiatric Association. (2013). *Diagnostic and statistical manual of mental disorders* (5th ed.). Washington, DC: Author.

Antonini, T. N., Becker, S. P., Tamm, L., & Epstein, J. N. (2015). Hot and cool executive functions in children with attention-deficit/hyperactivity disorder and comorbid oppositional defiant disorder. *Journal of the International Neuropsychological Society, 21*(8), 584-595.

Avisar, A. (2011). Which personality and behavioral characteristics are associated with difficulties in selective attention? *Journal of attention disorders, 15*(5), 357-67.

Avisar, A. (2014). *The experience of adolescents diagnosed with ADHD.* The Hebrew Psychology website, Retrieved from https://www.hebpsy.net/articles.asp?id=3196

Avisar, A. & Lavie-Ajayi, M. (2014). Listening to stories of Adolescents with ADHD About stimulant medication use. *Ethical Human Psychology and Psychiatry, 16*(1), 37-50.

Avisar, A. & Shalev, L. (2011). Sustained attention and behavioral characteristics associated with ADHD in adults. *Applied Neuropsychology, 18*(2), 107-16.

Banich, M. T. (2010). Brain imaging of the neural systems affected in adults with attention deficit/hyperactivity disorder. *Expert Review of Neurotherapeutics, 10*(10), 1523-7.

Barkley, R. A. (1997). Behavioral inhibition, sustained attention and executive functioning: Constructing a unifying theory of ADHD. *Psychological Bulletin, 121,* 65–94.

Baving, L., Rellum, T., Laucht, M., & Schmidt, M. H. (2016). Children with oppositional-defiant disorder display deviant attentional processing independent of ADHD symptoms. *Journal of Neural Transmission, 113*(5), 685-93.

Beau-Lejdstrom, R., Douglas, I., Evans, S. J., & Smeeth, L. (2016). Latest trends in ADHD drug prescribing patterns in children in the UK: prevalence, incidence and persistence. *BMJ Open, 6*(6), 1-8.

Bédard, M. J., Joyala, C. C., Godbouta, L., & Chantal, S. (2009). Executive functions and the obsessive-compulsive disorder: On the importance of subclinical symptoms and other concomitant factors. *Archives of Clinical Neuropsychology, 24*(6), 585-598.

Bender, W. N., & Smith, J. K. (1990). Classroom behavior of children and adolescents with learning disabilities: A meta-analysis. *Journal of Learning Disabilities, 23*(5), 298-305.

Berger, I., & Cassuto, H. (2014). The effect of environmental distractors incorporation into a CPT on sustained attention and ADHD diagnosis among adolescents. *Journal of Neuroscience Methods, 30,* 62-68.

Beyers, R. N. (2009). A five dimensional model for educating the net generation. *Educational Technology & Society, 12*(4), 218–227.

Biederman,J., & Faraone S. V. (2005). Attention deficit hyperactivity disorder. *The Lancet, 366,* 237-248.

Biederman, J., Newcorn, J., &Sprich, S. (1991). Comorbidity of attention deficit hyperactivity disorder with conduct, depressive, anxiety, and other disorders. *American Journal of Psychiatry,148,* 564–577.

Biederman, J., Spencer, T. J.,Newcorn, J. H., Gao, H., Milton, D. R., Feldman, P. D.,& Witte, M. M. (2007). Effect of comorbid symptoms of oppositional defiant disorder on responses to atomoxetine in children with ADHD: a meta-analysis of controlled clinical trial data. *Psychopharmacology, 190,* 31–41.

Birmaher, B., Ryan, N. D., & Williamson D. E. (1996). Childhood and adolescent depression: a review of the past 10 years, part I. *Journal of the American Academy of Child & Adolescent Psychiatry, 35,* 1427 -1439.

Boxhoorn, S., Lopez, E., Schmidt, C., Schulze, D., Hänig, S., & Freitag, C. (2018). Attention profiles in autism spectrum disorder and subtypes of attention-deficit/hyperactivity disorder. *European Child & Adolescent Psychiatry, 27*(11), 1433-1447.

Brodeur, D. A., & Pond, M. (2001). The development of selective attention in children with attention deficit hyperactivity disorder. *Journal of Abnormal Child Psychology, 29*, 229-239.

Brunsvold, G. I., Oepen, G., Federman, E. J., & Akins, R . (2008). Comorbid depression and ADHD in children and adolescents: consensus and controversy. *Psychiatric Times, 8*, 13-17.

Buitelaar, J. K., Van der Gaag, R. J., Swaab–Barneveld, H., & Kuiper, M. (1995). Prediction of clinical response to methylphenidate in children with attention-deficit hyperactivity disorder. *Journal of the American Academy of Child & Adolescent Psychiatry ,34*, 1025–1032.

Cairncross, M., & Miller, C. J. (2016). The effectiveness of mindfulness-based therapies for ADHD: a Meta-analytic review. *Journal of Attention Disorders*, doi: 10.1177/1087054715625301.

Castellanos, F. X., & Tannock, R. (2002). Neuroscience of attention-deficit/hyperactivity disorder: the search for endophenotypes. *Nature Reviews Neuroscience, 3*(8), 617-28.

Coghill, D. (2010). The impact of medications on quality of life in Attention-Deficit Hyperactivity Disorder: A systematic review. *CNS Drugs, 24*(10), 843-66.

Cohen, R., Senecky, Y., Shuper, A., Inbar, D., Chodick, G., Shalev, V., & Raz, R. (2013). Prevalence of epilepsy and attention-deficit hyperactivity (ADHD) disorder: A population - based study. *Journal of Child Neurology, 28*, 120-123.

Cohen, Y., Lachenmeyer, J.R., and Springer, C. (2003). Anxiety and selective attention in obsessive–compulsive disorder. *Behavior Research and Therapy, 41*, 1311–1323.

Conners, C.K. (2008). *Conners Comprehensive Behavior Rating Scale Manual*. Toronto, Ontario, Canada: Multi-Health Systems.

Cortese, S., Kelly, Clare., Chabernaud, C., Proal, E., Di, M. A., Milham, M. P., & Castellanos, F. X. (2012). Toward systems neuroscience of ADHD: A meta-analysis of 55 FMRI studies. *The American Journal of Psychiatry, 169*(10), 1038-55.

Daly, B. P., Creed, T., Xanthopoulos, M., & Brown, R. T. (2007). Psychosocial treatments for children with attention deficit/hyperactivity disorder. *Neuropsychology Review, 17*(1), 73-89.

Danielson, M. L., Bitsko, R. H., Ghandour, R. M., Holbrook, J. R., Kogan, M. D., & Blumberg, S. J. (2018). Prevalence of parent-reported ADHD diagnosis and associated treatment among U.S. children and adolescents, 2016. *Journal of Clinical Child and Adolescent Psychology, 47*(2), 199-212.

Douglas, V. I. (1972). Stop, look and listen: The problem of sustained attention and impulse control in hyperactive and normal children. *Canadian Journal of Behavior Science, 4*, 259–282.

Doyle, A., Biederman, J., Seidman, L. J., Reske-Nielsen, J. J., & Faraone, S. (2005). Neuropsychological functioning in relatives of girls with and without ADHD. *Psychological Medicine, 35*(8), 1121-32.

Dubey, D. R., & O'Leary, S. G. (1975). Increasing reading comprehension of two hyperactive children: Preliminary investigation. *Perceptual and Motor Skills, 41*, 691–694.

DuPaul, G. J., & Eckert, T. L. (1997). The effects of school-based interventions for Attention Deficit Hyperactivity Disorder: a meta analysis. *School Psychology Review, 26*, 5–27.

Efron, D., Jarman, F. C., & Barker, M. (1998). Child and parent perceptions of stimulants medication treatment in attention deficit hyperactivity disorder. *Journal of Paediatrics and Child Health, 34*, 288–292.

Epstein, J. N., Erkanli, A., Conners, C. K., Klaric, J., Costello, J. E., & Angold, A. (2003). Relations between continuous performance test performance measures and ADHD behaviors. *Journal of Abnormal Child Psychology, 1,* 543-554.

Epstein, J. N., Goldberg, N. A., Conners, C. K., & March, J. S. (1997). The effects of anxiety on continuous performance test functioning in an ADHD clinic sample. *Journal of Attention Disorders*, *2*(1), 45-52.

Epstein, J. N., Johnson, D. E., Varia, I. M., &Conners, C. K. (2001).Neuropsychological assessment of response inhibition in adults with ADHD. *Journal of Clinical and Experimental Neuropsychology, 23*, 362-371.

Ercan, E. S., Suren, S., Bacanli, A., Yazici, K., U., Calli, C., Ozyurt. O...Rohde, L. A. (2016). Decreasing ADHD phenotypic heterogeneity: searching for neurobiological underpinnings of the restrictive inattentive phenotype. *European Child & Adolescent Psychiatry, 25*(3), 273-282.

Evans, S. W., & Pelham, W. E. (2001). Psychostimulant effects on academic and behavioral measures for ADHD junior high school students in a lecture format classroom. *Journal of Abnormal Child Psychology, 19*, 537–552.

Eysenck, H.J. (1967). *The biological basis of personality*. Springfield, IL: Charles C.Thomas.

Factor, P. I., Reyes, R., & Rosen, P. J. (2014). Emotional impulsivity in children with ADHD associated with comorbid--not ADHD—symptomatology. *Journal of Psychopathology and Behavioral Assessment, 36*(4), 530-541.

Faraone, S. V., Perlis, R. H., Doyle, A. E., Smoller, J. W., Goralnick, J. J., Holmgren, M. A., & Sklar, P. (2005). Molecular genetics of attention-deficit/hyperactivity disorder. *Biological Psychiatry, 57*(11), 1313–1323.

Fehlings, D. L. (1991). Attention deficit hyperactivity disorder: does cognitive behavioral therapy improve home behavior? *Journal of Developmental and Behavioral Pediatrics, 12*, 223-228.

Fogelman, Y., Vinker, S., Guy, N., & Kahan, E. (2003). Prevalence of and change in the prescription of methylphenidate in Israel over a 2-year period. *CNS Drugs, 17*(12), 915-9.

Frankel, F., Myatt, R., Cantwell, D. P., & Feinberg,D. T. (1997). Parent assisted transfer of children's social skills training: Effects on children with and without attention-deficit hyperactivity disorder. *Journal of the American Academy of Child and Adolescent Psychiatry, 36*, 1056–1064.

Furman, L. (2005). What is attention-deficit hyperactivity disorder (ADHD)? *Journal of Child Neurology, 20,* 994-1002.

Gardner, B. K., Sheppard, D., & Efron, D. (2008). The impact of stimulants on a clinical measure of attention in children with ADHD. *Child Neuropsychology, 14*, 171-86.

Gaub, M., & Carlson, C. L. (1997). Behavioral characteristics of DSM IV ADHD subtypes in a school-based population. *Journal of Abnormal Child Psychology, 25,* 103–112.

Gittelman, R., Klein, D. F., & Feingold, I. (1983). Children with reading disorders—II. Effects of methylphenidate in combination with reading disabilities. *Journal of Child Psychology and Psychiatry, 24*, 193–212.

Goldstein, S., & Gordon, M. (2003). Gender issues and ADHD: Sorting fact from fiction. The ADHD Report, 11(4), 7-16.

Greenberg, L.M. (1996). *Test of Variables of Attention.* Los Alamitos: University Attention Disorder Inc.

Greven, C. U., Asherton, P., Rijsdijk, F. V., & Plomin, R. (2011). A longitudinal twin study on the association between inattentive and hyperactive-impulsive ADHD symptoms. *Journal of Abnormal Child Psychology, 39*, 623-632.

Grizenko, N., Bhat, M., Schwartz, G., Ter-Stepanian, M., & Joober, R. (2006). Efficacy of methylphenidate in children with attention-deficit hyperactivity disorder and learning disabilities: a randomized crossover trial. *Journal of Psychiatry & Neuroscience, 31*(1), 46–51.

Hails, K. A., Zhou, Y., & Shaw, D. S. (2019). The mediating effect of self-regulation in the association between poverty and child weight: a systematic review. *Clinical Child and Family Psychology Review, 22*(3), 290-315.

Hall, C. L.,Valentine, A. Z., Groom, M. J., Walker, G. M., & Sayal, K. (2016). The clinical utility of the continuous performance test and objective measures of activity for diagnosing and monitoring ADHD in children: a systematic review. *European Child & Adolescent Psychiatry 25*(7), 677-699.

Harpur, R. A., Thompson, M., Daley, D., Abikoff, H., & Sonuga-Barke, E. J. S. (2008). The Attention-Deficit/Hyperactivity Disorder medication-related attitudes of patients and their parents. *Journal of Child and Adolescent Psychopharmacology, 18*(5), 461-473.

Hart, H., Radua, J., Nakao, T.,Mataix-Cols, D., & Rubia, K. (2013). Meta-analysis of functional magnetic resonance imaging studies of inhibition and attention in attention-deficit/hyperactivity disorder: Exploring task-specific, stimulant medication, and age effects .*JAMA Psychiatry, 70*, 185-198.

Hazell, P. (2003). Depression in children and adolescents. *Evidence - Based Mental Health, 6*(4), 103.

Hazell, P. (2007). Pharmacological management of attention-deficit hyperactivity disorder in adolescents—Special considerations. *CNS Drugs, 21*, 37–4.

Hazell, P. L., Carr, V. J., Lewin, T. J., Dewis, S. A. M., Heathcote, D. M., & Brucki, B. M. (1999). Effortful and automatic processing in boys with ADHD and specific learning disorders. *Journal of Child Psychology and Psychiatry, 40*, 275-286.

Hervey, A. S., Epstein, J. N., &Cury, J. F. (2004). Neuropsychology of adults with attention-deficit/hyperactivity disorder: A

Meta-Analytic Review. *Neuropsychology, 18(3),* 485-503.

Hobson C.W., Scott S., & Rubia K. (2011). Investigation of cool and hot executive function in ODD/CD independently of ADHD. *Journal of Child Psychology and Psychiatry, 52*(10), 1035-1043.

Holden, S., Jenkins-Jones, S., Poole, D. C., Morgan, C., Coghill, D., & Currie, C. J. (2013). The prevalence and incidence, resource use and financial costs of treating people with attention deficit/hyperactivity disorder (ADHD) in the United Kingdom (1998 to 2010). *Child and Adolescent Psychiatry and Mental Health, 7,* 20–34.

Holland, J., & Sayal, K. (2019). Relative age and ADHD symptoms, diagnosis and medication: a systematic review. *European Child & Adolescent Psychiatry, 28*(11), 1417-1429. DOI:10.1007/s00787-018-1229-6

Holler, K., Kavanaugh, B., & Cook, N. E. (2014). Executive functioning in adolescent depressive disorders. *Journal of Child and Family Studies, 23(*8), 1315-1324.

Hopwood C. J., & Morey, L. C. (2008). Emotional problems suppress disorder/performance associations in adult ADHD assessment. *Journal of Psychopathology and Behavioral Assessments, 30,* 204-210.

Hoza, B., Mrug, S., Pelham, W. E. Jr., Greiner, A. R., & Gnagy, E. M. (2003). A friendship intervention for children with Attention-Deficit/Hyperactivity Disorder: preliminary findings. *Journal of Attention Disorders, 6,* 87–98.

Hoza, B., Owens, J. S., Pelham, W. E., Swanson, J. M., Conners, C. K., Hinshaw, S. P... Kraemer, H. C. (2000). Parent cognitions as predictors of child treatment response in attention-deficit/hyperactivity disorder. *Journal of Abnormal Child Psychology, 28,* 569–583.

Huang, Y., & Tsai, M. (2011). Long-Term Outcomes with Medications for Attention-Deficit Hyperactivity Disorder. *CNS Drugs, 25*(7), 539-54.

Huang-Pollock, C. L., Nigg, J. T., and Carr, T. H. (2005). Deficient attention is hard to find: applying the perceptual load model of selective attention to attention deficit hyperactivity disorder subtypes. *Journal of Child Psychology and Psychiatry, 46*, 1211-1218.

Humphreys K. L., & Lee, S. S. (2011). Risk taking and sensitivity to punishment in children with ADHD, ODD, ADHD+ODD, and controls. *Journal of Psychopathology and Behavioral Assessment, 33*(3), 299-307

Humphreys, K. L., Watts, E. L., Dennis, E. L., King, L. S., Thompson, P. M., & Gotlib, I. H. (2019). Stressful life events, ADHD symptoms, and brain structure in early adolescence. *Journal of Abnormal Child Psychology, 47*(3), 421-432.

International Classification of Diseases, Tenth Revision, Clinical Modification (ICD-10-CM)". National Center for Health Statistics. Centers for Disease Control and Prevention (CDC). version 2015 retrieved 2017.

Jarrett, M. A., & Ollendick, T. H. (2008). A conceptual review of the comorbidity of attention-deficit/hyperactivity disorder and anxiety: Implications for future research and practice. *Clinical Psychology Review 28*, 1266–1280.

Johnson, K. A., Kelly S. P., Bellgrove, M. A., Barry, A., Cox, M., Gill, M., & Robertson, I. H. (2007). Response variability in Attention Deficit Hyperactivity Disorder: Evidence for neuropsychological heterogeneity. *Neuropsychologia, 45*, 630-638.

Kavale, K. A., & Forness, S. R. (1996). Social skill deficits and learning disabilities: A meta-analysis. *Journal of Learning Disabilities, 29*(3), 226-237.

Kellner, J.A. (2013). *75% of the students are taking Ritalin - no prescription.* Retrieved from https://www.ynet.co.il/articles/0,7340,L-4467268,00.html

Kim, E., Song, J., Kyeong, S., & Lee, S. B. (2016). 6.58 Subgroups identification of attention-deficit/hyperactivity disorder in dimensions of symptoms severity and intelligence using topological data analysis and their functional network modular organizations. *Journal of the American Academy of Child and Adolescent Psychiatry, 55*(10), 223.

Knouse, L. E., Teller, J., &Brooks, M. A. (2017). Meta-analysis of cognitive-behavioural treatments for adult ADHD. *Journal of Consulting and Clinical Psychology, 85*, 737-750.

Kroese, J. M., Hynd, G. W., Knight, D. F., Hiemenz, J. R., & Hall, J. (2000). Clinical appraisal of spelling ability and its relationship to phonemic awareness (blending, segmenting, elision, and reversal), phonological memory, and reading in reading disabled, ADHD, and normal children. *Reading and Writing: An Interdisciplinary Journal, 13*, 105-131.

Kube, D. A., Petersen, M.C., & Palmer, F. B. (2002). Attention deficit hyperactivity disorder: comorbidity and medication use. *Clinical Pediatric, 41*(7), 461-9.

Lahey, B. B., & Carlson, C. L. (1992). *Validity of the diagnostic category of attention deficit disorder without hyperactivity: A review of the literature.* In S. E. Shaywitz & B. A. Shaywitz (Eds.), Attention deficit disorder comes of age: Toward the twenty-first century (pp. 119–144). Austin, TX: Pro-Ed.

Landau, S., & Moore, L. A. (1991). Social skill deficits in children with attention deficit/hyperactivity disorder. *School Psychology Review, 20*, 235–251.

LeFever, G. B., Dawson, K. V., & Morrow, A. L. (1999). The extent of drug therapy for attention deficit-hyperactivity disorder among children in public schools. *American Journal of Public Health, 89*(9), 1359-64.

Lima, R. F., Azoni, C. A. S., Ciasca, S. M. (2011). Attentional performance and executive functions in children with learning difficulties. *Psicologia, Reflexão e Crítica, 24*(4), 685-691.

Lindstrøm, J. A. (2012). Why attention-deficit/hyperactivity disorder is not a true medical syndrome. *Ethical Human Psychology and Psychiatry, 14*(1), 61-73.

Livingstone, L. T., Coventry, W. L., Corley, R. P., Willcutt, E. G., Samuelsson, S., Olson, R. K., & Byrne, B. (2016). Does the Environment Have an Enduring Effect on ADHD? A Longitudinal Study of Monozygotic Twin Differences in Children. *Journal of Abnormal Child Psychology, 44*(8), 1487-1501.

Lundahl, B., Risser, H. J., & Lovejoy, C. (2006). A meta-analysis of parent training: Moderators and follow-up effects. *Clinical Psychology Review, 26*, 86–104.

Machlin, L., McLaughlin, K. A., & Sheridan, M. A. (2020). Brain structure mediates the association between socioeconomic status and attention-deficit/hyperactivity disorder. *Developmental Science, 23*(1). DOI: 10.1111/desc.12844

Martel, M. M., Nigg, J. T., & Lucas, R. E. (2008). Trait mechanisms in youth with and without attention-deficit/hyperactivity disorder. *Journal of Research in Personality, 42*, 895–913.

Mayes, S. D., Calhoun, S. L., & Crowell, E. W. (2000). Learning disabilities and ADHD: Overlapping spectrum disorders. *Journal of Learning Disabilities, 33*(5), 417-424.

McDermott, L. M., & Ebmeier, K. P. (2009). A meta-analysis of depression severity and cognitive function. *Journal of Affective Disorders, 119*, 1-8.

McNeal, R. E., Roberts, M. C., & Barone, V. J. (2000). Mothers' and children's perceptions of medication for children with attention-deficit hyperactivity disorder. *Child Psychiatry & Human Development, 30*, 173–187.

Meaux, J. B., Hester, C., Smith, B., & Shoptaw, A. (2006). Stimulant medications: A trade-off? The lived experience of adolescents with ADHD. *Journal for Specialists in Pediatric Nursing, 11*(4), 214-226.

Ministry of Health. (2010). *Criteria for diagnosing ADHD in children, adolescents and adults.* Circular No. 40/2010, retrieved from https://www.health.gov.il/hozer/mr40_2010.pdf

Monuteaux, M. C., Faraone, S. V., Herzig, K., Navsaria, N., &Biederman, J. (2005). ADHD and Dyscalculia: Evidence for Independent Familial Transmission. *Journal of Learning Disabilities, 38*(1). 86-93.

Neudecker,C., Mewes, N., Reimers, A. K., & Woll, A. (2019). Exercise interventions in children and adolescents with ADHD: a systematic review. *Journal of attention disorders, 23*(4), 307-324.

Newlove-Delgado, T., Ford, T. J., Hamilton, W., Janssens, A., & Stein, K. (2019). Resumption of attention-deficit hyperactivity disorder medication in early adulthood: findings from a UK primary care prescribing study. *European Child & Adolescent Psychiatry, 28*(12), 1589-1596. DOI: 10.1007/s00787-019-01325-5

Nigg, J. T., Blaskey, L. G., Huang-Pollock, C. L., Hinshaw, S. P., John, O. P., Willcutt, E. G., & Pennington, B. (2002). Big Five dimensions and ADHD symptoms: Links between personality traits and clinical symptoms. *Journal of Personality and Social Psychology, 83*(2), 451–469.

Nixon, E. (2001). The social competence of children with attention deficit hyperactivity disorder: a review of the literature. *Child Psychology and Psychiatry Review, 6*, 172 -180.

Nomura, Y., Wickramaratne, P. J., Pilowsky, D. J., Newcorn, J. H., Bruder-Costello, B., Davey, c...Weissman, M. M. (2007).

Low birth weight and risk of affective disorders and selected medical illness in offspring at high and low risk for depression. *Comprehensive Psychiatry, 48*(5), 470-478.

O'Hearn, K., Asato, M., Ordaz,S., & Luna, B. (2008). Neurodevelopment and executive function in autism. *Development and Psychopathology, 20*(4), 1103-32.

Oldehinkel, M., Francx, W., Beckmann, C. F., Buitelaar, J. K., &Mennes, M. (2013). Resting state FMRI research in child psychiatric disorders. *European Child & Adolescent Psychiatry, 22*(12), 757-70.

O'Neill, M. E., & Douglas, V. I., (1991). Study strategies and story recall in attention deficit disorder and reading disability. *Journal of Abnormal Child Psychology, 19*, 671-692.

Ornoy, A., Ovadia, M., Rivkin, D., Milshtein, E., &Barlev, L. (2016). Prevalence of ADHD among 7-9-year-old children in Israel. A comparison between Jewish and Arab populations. *The Israel Journal of Psychiatry and Related Sciences, 53*(2), 3-9.

Overmeyer, S., & Taylor, E. (1999). Principles for treating hyperkinetic disorder: practice approaches for the UK. *Journal of Child Psychology and Psychiatry, 40*, 1147-1157.

Phan, K.L., Wagner, T.D., Taylor, S.F., & Liberzon, I. (2004). Functioning neuro imaging studies of human emotions. *CNS Spectrums, 9*(4), 258-266.

Pietrzak, R. H,, Mollica, C. M., Maruff, P., & Snyder, P. J. (2006). Cognitive effects of immediate-release methylphenidate in children with attention-deficit/hyperactivity disorder. *Neuroscience & Biobehavioral Reviews, 30*, 1225-45.

Pitcher, T. M., Piek., J. P., & Hay, D. A. (2003). Fine and gross motor ability in males with ADHD. *Developmental Medicine and Child Neurology, 45*(8), 525-35.

Pliszka, S. R. (1989). Effect of anxiety on cognition, behavior, and stimulant response in ADHD. *Journal of the American Academy of Child & Adolescent Psychiatry, 28*, 882–887.

Poissant, H., Mendrek, A., Talbot, N., Khoury, B., & Nolan, J. (2019). Behavioral and cognitive impacts of mindfulness-based interventions on adults with attention-deficit hyperactivity disorder: a systematic review. *Behavioural Neurology*, doi: 10.1155/2019/5682050.

Polanczyk, G., Silva de Lima, M., Bernardo, L., Biederman, J.,&Rohde, L. A. (2010). The worldwide prevalence of ADHD: A systematic review and meta regression Analysis. *The American Journal of Psychiatry, 164, 6*, 942-8.

Posserud, M., Ullebø, A. K., Plessen, K. J., Stormark, K. M., Gillberg, C. & Lundervold, A. J. (2014). Influence of assessment instrument on ADHD diagnosis. *European Child & Adolescent Psychiatry, 23*(4), 197-205 .

Poulin, C. (2007). From attention-deficit/hyperactivity disorder to medical stimulant use to the diversion of prescribed stimulants to non-medical stimulant use: connecting the dots. *Addiction, 102*, 740–751.

Powers, R. L., Marks, D. J., Miller, C. J., Newcorn, J. H., & Halperin, J. M. (2008). Stimulant treatment in children with Attention-Deficit/Hyperactivity Disorder moderates adolescent academic outcome. *Journal of Child and Adolescent Psychopharmacology, 18*, 449–459.

Price, A., Ford, T., Janssens, A., Williams, A. J., & Newlove-Delgado, T. (2020). Regional analysis of UK primary care prescribing and adult service referrals for young people with attention-deficit hyperactivity disorder. The British Journal of Psychiatry (BJPsych), 6(1). DOI:10.1192/bjo.2019.94

Pritchard, V. E., Neumann, E., & Rucklidge, J. J. (2008). Selective attention and inhibitory deficits in ADHD: Does subtype or comorbidity modulate negative priming effects? *Brain and Cognition, 67*, 324-339.

Rapoport, J. L., Buchsbaum, M. S., Weingarter, H., Zahn, P., Ludlow, C., & Mikkelsen, E. J. (1980). Dextroamphetamine: cognitive and behavioural effects in normal and hyperactive boys and normal men. *Archives of General Psychiatry, 37*, 933- 943.

Rasmussen, N. (2008). *On speed: The many lives of amphetamine.* New York, NY: New York University Press.

Reinholdt-Dunne, M. L., Mogg, K., Vangkilde, S. A., Bradley, B. P., & Esbjørn, B. H. (2015). Attention control and attention to emotional stimuli in anxious children before and after cognitive behavioral therapy. *Cognitive Therapy and Research, 39*, 785–796.

Riccio, C., Waldrop, J.J, Reynolds, C.R., & Lowe, P. (2001). Effects of stimulants on the continuous performance test (CPT): Implications for CPT use and interpretation. *The Journal of Neuropsychiatry and Clinical Neurosciences, 13*(3), 326-35.

Rowland, A. S., Umbach, D. M., Stallone, L., Naftel, J., Bohlig, M., & Sandler, D. P. (2002). Prevalence of medication treatment for attention-deficit/hyperactivity disorder among elementary school children in Johnston County, North Carolina. *American Journal of Public Health, 92*, 231–234.

Rubia, Katya., Alegria, Analucia., & Brinson, Helen. (2014). Imaging the ADHD brain: disorder-specificity, medication effects and clinical translation. *Expert Review of Neurotherapeutics, 14*(5), 519-38.

Rubin, K. H., Bukowski, W., & Parker, J. G. (1998). *Peer interactions, relationships, and groups.* In W. Damon (Series Ed.) & N. Eisenberg (Vol. Ed.), *Handbook of child psychology: Social, emotional, and personality development* (Vol. 3, pp. 619–700). New York: Wiley.

Santosh, P. J., & Taylor, E. (2000). Stimulant drugs. *European Child & Adolescent Psychiatry, 9*(I), 27-43.

Schwartz, A. (2013). The Selling of Attention Deficit Disorder. Retrieved on 15/3/2018 from http://www.nytimes.com/2013/12/15/health/the-selling-of-attention-deficit-disorder.html

Seidman, L. J. (2006). Neuropsychological functioning in people with ADHD across the lifespan. *Clinical Psychology Review, 26*, 466-485.

Seidman, L. J., Biederman, J., Monteaux, M. C., Valera, E., Doyle, A. E., & Faraone, S. V. (2005). Impact of Gender and Age on Executive Functioning: Do Girls and boys with and without Attention Deficit Hyperactivity Disorder Differ Neuropsychologically in Preteen and Teenage Years? *Developmental Neuropsychology, 27*(1), 79-105.

Semrud-clikeman, M., Walkowiak, J., Wilkinson, A., &Minne, E. P. (2010). Direct and indirect measures of social perception, behavior, and emotional functioning in children with asperger's disorder, nonverbal learning disability, or ADHD. *Journal of Abnormal Child Psychology, 38*(4), 509-519.

Skogli, E. W., Egeland J., Andersen P. N., Hovik K. T., & Øie, M. (2014). Few differences in hot and cool executive functions in children and adolescents with combined and inattentive subtypes of ADHD. *Child Neuropsychology, 20*, 162-18.

Smith, J. A., Flowers, J., & Larkin, M. (2009). *Interpretative phenomenological* analysis*: Theory, method and research.* London, United Kingdom: Sage.

Smith, M. E., Farah, M. J. (2011). Are prescription stimulants "smart pills"? The epidemiology and cognitive neuroscience of prescription stimulant use by normal healthy individuals. *Psychological Bulletin, 137*, 717–741.

Smith, T. E., Lee, C. A., Martel, M. M., &Axelrad, M. E. (2017). ODD symptom network during preschool. *Journal of Abnormal Child Psychology, 45*(4), 743-748.

Sonuga-Barke, E.J. (2003). The dual pathway model of AD/HD: An elaboration of neuro-developmental characteristics. *Neuroscience & Biobehavioral Reviews, 27*(7), 593-604.

Stergiakouli, Evie., George, D. S., Martin, Joanna., Skuse, D. H., Viechtbauer, Wolfgang., Ring., S. M... Pourcain, B. (2017). Shared genetic influences between dimensional ASD and ADHD symptoms during child and adolescent development. *Molecular Autism, 8*(18), DOI 10.1186/s13229-017-0131-2.

Swanson, J. M., Baler, R. D., & Volkow, N. D. (2011). Understanding the effects of stimulant medications on cognition in individuals with Attention-Deficit Hyperactivity Disorder: A decade of progress. *Neuropsychopharmacology Reviews, 36*, 207–226.

Swanson, J. M., Kraemer, H. C., Hinshaw, S. P., Arnold, L.E., Conners, C. K., & Wigal, T. (2001). Clinical relevance of the primary findings of the MTA: Success rates based on severity of ADHD and ODD symptoms at the end of treatment. *Journal of the American Academy of Child & Adolescent Psychiatry, 40*, 168–179.

Swanson, J. M., Wigal, S. B., Wigal, T., Sonuga-Barge, E., Greenhill, L. L., Biederman, J...Hatch, S. J. (2004). A comparison of once-daily extended-release methylphenidate formulations in children with attention-deficit/hyperactivity disorder in the laboratory school (the comacs Study). *Pediatrics 113*, 206–216.

Tannock, R. (2000). *Attention-deficit/hyperactivity disorder with anxiety disorders.* In T. E. Brown (Ed.), Attention-deficit disorders and comorbidities in children, adolescents, and adults (pp. 125–170). Washington, DC: American Psychiatric Press.

The Marker, retrieved from the New York Times article. (2013). *is there an epidemic of attention deficit disorder or are drug manufacturers trying to make money? A two-decade campaign of drug companies among doctors, teachers and parents has resulted in a five-fold increase in sales of ADHD drugs.* Retrieved from https://www.themarker.com/wallstreet/1.2196119

Tsal, Y., Shalev, L., & Mevorach, C. (2005). The diversity of attention deficits in ADHD: the prevalence of four cognitive factors in ADHD versus controls. *Journal of Learning Disabilities, 38*(2), 142-57.

Van der Meere, J., and Sergeant, J. (1988). Focused attention in pervasively hyperactive children. *Journal of Abnormal Child Psychology, 16,* 627-639.

Van Der Schans, J., Cicek, R., Vardar, S., Bos, H. J., de Vries, T. W., Hoekstra, P. J., & Hak, E. (2017). Methylphenidate use and school performance among primary school children: a descriptive study. *BMC Psychiatry, 17*(116), 1-9.

Van, D. J., Arns, M., Heinrich, H., Vollebregt, M., Strehl, U., & Loo, K. S. (2019). Sustained effects of neurofeedback in ADHD: a systematic review and meta-analysis. *European Child and Adolescent Psychiatry, 28*(3), 293-305.

Vinker, S., Vinker, R., & Elhayany, A. (2006). Prevalence of Methylphenidate Use among Israeli Children. *Clinical Drug Investigation, 26*(3), 161-167.

Vlam, S. L. (2006), Attention-deficit/hyperactivity disorder: Diagnostic assessment methods used by advanced practice registered nurses. *Pediatric Nursing, 32*(1), 18-25.

Wang, L. J., Huang, Y. S., Chiang, Y. L., Hsiao, C. C., Shang, Z. Y., & Chen, C. K. (2011). Clinical symptoms and performance on the continuous performance test in children with attention deficit hyperactivity disorder between subtypes: a natural follow-up study for 6 months. *BMC Psychiatry, 11*, 65-72.

Ward, M.F., Wender, P.H., & Remherr, F.W. (1993). The Wender Utah Rating Scale: an aid in the retrospective diagnosis of childhood attention deficit hyperactivity disorder. *American Journal of Psychiatry,* 150, 885-890.

Watson, G. L., Arcona, A. P., & Antonuccio, D. O. (2015). The ADHD drug abuse crisis on American college campuses. *Ethical Human Psychology and Psychiatry, 17*(1), 5-21.

Wei, X., Yu, J. W., & Shaver, D. (2014). Longitudinal effects of ADHD in children with learning disabilities or emotional disturbances. *Exceptional Children, 80*(2), 205-219.

White, J. D. (1999). Personality temperament and ADHD: A review of the literature. *Personality and Individual Differences, 27*, 589–598.

Wienersky, A. (2018). *ADHD and athletic performance.* Retrieved from https://www.wingate.org.il/Index.asp?ArticleID=6831 &CategoryID=105

Willcutt, E. G., Nigg, J. T., Pennington, B. F., Solanto, M. V., Rohde, L. A., Tannock, R... Lahey B. B. (2012). Validity of DSM-IV attention deficit/hyperactivity disorder symptom dimensions and subtypes. *Journal of Abnormal Psychology, 121*(4), 991-110.

Wolraich, M. L. (2003). Annotation: The use of psychotropic medications in children: An American view. *Journal of Child Psychology and Psychiatry, 44*, 159–168.

Yang, B. R., Chan R. C. K., Gracia N., Cao X. Y., Zou X. B., Jing J., & Shum D. (2011). Cool and hot executive functions in medication-naive attention deficit hyperactivity disorder children. *Psychological Medicine, 41*(12), 2593-2602.

Zentall, S. S., & Leib, S. L. (1985). Structured tasks: Effects on activity and performance of hyperactive and comparison children. *Journal of Educational Research, 79*, 91–95.

Zhan, C., Liu, Y., Wu, K., Gao, Y., & Li, X. (2017). Structural and functional abnormalities in children with Attention-Deficit/Hyperactivity Disorder: A focus on subgenual anterior cingulate cortex. *Brain Connectivity, 7*(2), 106-114.

index

W

weight, 56, 57, 63, 93, 133, 139